Living The Code

Always
Live
The
Code

DAKOTA

Living The Code

SEVEN PRINCIPLES THAT
COULD CHANGE YOUR LIFE

DAKOTA LIVESAY

Library of Congress Control Number: 2012912842
ISBN: Hardcover   978-1-4771-4568-5
                 Softcover   978-1-4771-4567-8
                 Ebook   978-1-4771-4569-2

This book was printed in the United States of America.

To order additional copies of this book, contact:
Xlibris Corporation
1-888-795-4274
www.Xlibris.com
Orders@Xlibris.com
115856

Contents

Acknowledgements

As I indicate in the Introduction, I have to acknowledge all the wise people over the centuries who I've never met, but their written and spoken words have inspired me to be the person I am today and hope to become in the future. This includes the recently departed Steven Covey.

Of the people close to me, I couldn't have even started the book, let alone finish it without the encouragement of my wife and best friend, Sunny.

I also want to thank Bill O'Neal for his introducing me to the importance of the American frontier in making the United States the great country it is today, and his assistance in my writing about the development of that frontier.

And a special thanks to Chip Cannon for providing those great illustrations that will keep you smiling throughout the book.

Chapter 1

Introduction

This book could very well be one of the most important books you will ever read. After reading that statement, I can hear you say, "Wow, is this guy conceited to think what he's written is that important?"

First, let me say, I don't consider myself the author of this book. I've just assembled this book from a lifetime of conversations with men and women of principle, theologians, historians, and educators, as well as my reading what these people have written.

As Dale Carnegie said, "The ideas I stand for are not mine. I borrowed them from Socrates. I swiped them from Chesterfield. I stole them from Jesus. And I put them in a book. If you don't like their rules, whose would you use?"

My hope is that as you read this book, you will be inspired to live your life in accordance with the seven principles explained. By doing so, you won't become a saint overnight or probably ever attain the level of sainthood. But I can assure you that as you do your best each day, each day you will become a better man, woman, boy, or girl. And your example will inspire others to do the same, which, in turn, will make this world a better place for all of us to live.

Each page of this book has been inspired by three words, without which our lives would not be complete. These words are faith, family, and freedom.

Most of my adult life I've been a writer. I've written a number of articles for magazines, I've had two syndicated newspaper columns, and since 1999, I've been the publisher of *Chronicle of the Old West*. But I've always maintained I would never put together a book. That's because traditionally once I write a couple thousand words, I get bored with the subject about which I'm writing.

At the same time, I've admired author friends who have spent a number of years researching and writing a specific book. I've always thought, *Now that's passion.*

Back in 2004, I started getting intrigued with what Zane Gray called the *Code* of the West. I began wondering what this country and even the whole world would be like if everyone tried to live by this "code."

As I studied them, I felt there were several of the principles that people today would wonder just what they meant. "Ride for the brand" was one.

So I gathered together the principles from all the sources I could find. Then I categorized them and restated them in words we could all understand. I came up with seven.

They include the following:

1. Respect yourself and others.
2. Accept responsibility for your life.
3. Be positive and cheerful.
4. Be a person of your word.
5. Go the distance.
6. Be fair in all your dealings.
7. Be a good friend and neighbor.

Chronicle of the Old West began giving certificates to people who committed to living by this code. Right now, these certificates are adorning the walls of homes, offices, and even classrooms around the world.

Periodically, we receive a request from someone in prison. We always thought it would be interesting if the certificate would be a part of the person's portfolio when they appeared before the parole board.

Next, I started writing essays, explaining my understanding of how these seven principles should be played out in our lives. I discovered I was developing a passion for sharing my interpretation of the code in much the same way my author friends did with the subjects about which they wrote. So I decided to assemble this book. When I finished it, I realized another principle about life: "Never say never."

Child prodigies who graduate from college at the age of sixteen always pursue a degree in a hard science such as mathematics, physics, or chemistry because human sciences require life's experience, which only age can bring about.

How many times have we said to someone "But you don't understand"? It might be we didn't do a good job of explaining. However, the chances are much greater the person we're talking to has no grasp (or life experience) of what we're talking about.

In assembling this book, I'm bringing over seventy years of life's experiences with many mistakes, failures, and even more successes.

Understand this book is going to require some astute thinking and decision-making on your part. We may believe we spend most of our time thinking. But are we really thinking, or are we remembering? When we "think" about the past either to reminisce about pleasant experiences, or to analyze non-pleasant ones, what we're really doing is remembering. Normally, when we "think" about concepts, we're really not thinking. What we're doing is remembering concepts we've been taught.

When we look at something in a different way, we're thinking. Thinking is creativity. It's approaching something unlike anyone else. *Orville Redenbacher didn't remember*, he thought. He took a lowly kernel of corn and started a whole new industry of gourmet popcorn. So from this point forward, I'm asking you to put on your thinking cap.

Few people would disagree that the United States is getting close to a collapse of values and ethics. Lying and cheating are OK as long as the person lying and cheating doesn't get caught at it. And if they do, it's OK as long as they're able to do a great job of apologizing.

In addition, when people do something unethical and get caught, they seek approval by being able to explain it wasn't really as bad as it seemed or that there are others who are much worse. I find it interesting how people can always find someone who is more unethical than they are. And it seems the more people who do it, the less unethical it is.

We live in a time of "grays." Nothing seems to be good or bad. There are no absolutes. I remember listening to a debate between two people about morality. One person maintained there were no absolutes. The other person took the side that there were absolutes in life. He said to his opponent, "Are you absolutely sure there are no absolutes?"

The other person responded, "Yes, definitely." Then he hesitated and, realizing he had just supported his opponent's theory, said, "Definitely not." Either way he lost. Logic says if there is one absolute in life, there are probably several more.

I don't believe life is totally black and white, but it's a lot more absolute than we see in the lives of most people today.

Right is right, and wrong is wrong. There is no free ride, and we must all pull together, or we'll fail together. We need to face up to our problems and meet them head-on. And let me tell you folks, there is no better time than right now.

Orison Sweet Marden, in a book he wrote in 1913 entitled *Training for Efficiency*, said the following. Incidentally, it's even more applicable today:

"Never before in the world's history have we stood upon the brink of such mighty things as we do today. All the past ages have been like a snowball rolling up to greatness. Today is a summing up of all the centuries. It is a storehouse into which the ages have poured their treasures. Every inventor, every discoverer, every thinker, every workman who has ever lived has contributed the results of his efforts to this day.

"Today is the biggest day in the world's history because it is made up of all the days that have gone before it, and in it are packed all the success, all the achievement, all the progress of the past. What a starting point for the youth compared with the corresponding date a century or even a half century ago!

"How we have been emancipated from drudgery by steam, by electricity, by the discoveries in chemistry, in physics! What immunity, what emancipation we have won from the discomforts and slavery of the past! The masses today have luxuries which the world's monarchs did not enjoy a century ago."

As Orison Marden says, we have opportunities today never realized by the people who came before us. But as long as we live lives with no moral compass, the opportunities will go by the wayside.

If you take this book seriously, it will change your life.

Chapter 2

Born on the Frontier

It's inconceivable that anyone raised in a country anywhere on this planet with any level of electronic communication has not heard about cowboys and America's Old West. And without a doubt, the vast majority of these people have at one time wanted to be cowboys themselves.

On any weekend, tens of thousands of men, women, and children dress up and pretend to be cowboys and cowgirls, as well as various characters from America's Western heritage. These are not kooks who have been let out of the local asylum for the weekend. These are businessmen, lawyers, doctors, blue-collar workers, housewives, and teachers. These are people like you and me who have become enthralled with the life of the Old West cowboy.

Just why do these sixteen to twenty-three-year-old boys—yes, that's their age—hold so much influence on us today? After asking scores of historians and Old West enthusiasts, I've come up with some ideas. Cowboys rode a horse, and historically, knights and nobility were the people who rode horses. Cowboys rode the open plains and were free and independent. Although Hollywood portrays the cowboy as being wild and ready to kill at the drop of a hat, the vast majority of the cowboys were young men with a high standard of ethics—something to be admired.

Incidentally, to judge all cowboys based on the misbehavior of a few would be the same as judging all college students based on the few who misbehave during spring break.

We've all heard of *The Code of the West*. As these men shared the hardships and dangers of roundups and cattle drives, as well as the loneliness of line shacks during the winter, it resulted in a special camaraderie and a society based on trust and interdependence. As a result, a series of informal principles came into play. These included the following: ride for the brand, don't inquire into a person's past, never pass anyone on the trail without saying "Howdy", and your word is your bond. And the list can go on and on. It was a gentleman's agreement to rules of conduct in one's life. It was something respected by everyone.

> "To judge all cowboys based on the misbehavior of a few would be the same as judging all college students based on the few who misbehave during spring break."

The time of the Old West cowboy was only about thirty years, and this code didn't start with them. The code started all the way back to 1620 when a group of people called pilgrims arrived on the American continent. They were religious dissidents who referred to themselves as "first comers." Incidentally, they were called pilgrims because they were on a religious journey or pilgrimage.

After starving that first year, they found that being a good neighbor with, rather than fighting, the Algonquian Indians, along with hard work, would result in success. We're all aware of that first Thanksgiving. Incidentally, unlike today's turkey and dressing, the food eaten at that first Thanksgiving was probably eel, clams, lobster, and venison.

It's interesting to note that although the pilgrims came to this "promised land" for religious freedom, they very well could have felt themselves failures because they were also hoping to find El Dorado, the golden city. What they found was a land that was mysterious, wild, and seemingly unconquerable. Unknown to them, they actually had found El Dorado. It was just that the wealth wasn't lying around for a person to reach down and pick up. The land had bountiful riches, but it required a unique people with unique characteristics to harvest those bountiful riches.

For the next three hundred years after those first pioneers arrived, the United States had a frontier. And it was on that frontier that men and women were challenged just to survive. It was the frontier that developed a people of determination, creativity, and cooperation. It was the frontier that drove these people to develop a great nation.

The frontier also developed a new sense of freedom. No longer was there a religion dictated by the government. In Europe, common people weren't allowed to own firearms. In this new land, firearms were essential for gathering meat and protecting one's family. So their ownership became a right. And with these additional rights came the necessity to accept personal responsibility in the expression of these rights.

Just Who Are These Pioneers?

They weren't the wealthy. The rich didn't migrate because they had businesses and property they didn't want to give up.

They weren't the poor because it wasn't cheap to outfit a family for travel. Wagons alone cost between $60 and $90. Animals to pull the wagon were also expensive. Then they needed provisions to get them to their destination and months afterward until they were able to get established.

The pioneers were middle-class, blue-collar people, typically in their twenties. They were dreamers who believed they ought to do better. And like the pilgrims who came across an ocean years before, they were on the move. It was in their blood.

> "The word impossible is peculiar because if you examine it closely, you'll find that most of it is possible."

Unlike the original pilgrims, later pioneers had the skills and the tools to build homes and survive. Those going to the rural frontier were often farmers or the sons of farmers. The pioneers who didn't want to be farmers came to support the farmers with skills like blacksmithing, harness making, and carpentry. There were also teachers, doctors, and even lawyers. They found that to survive, it took honesty and neighborly charity.

Traveling to the latest frontier was a great time for men. They were able to display their independence, creativity, and ingenuity. Women typically went to the frontier to be with their husbands. And the time when they were migrating was at the height of their childbearing years. They were often carrying an infant inside them or in their arms. The many unmarked children's graves alongside the trails testified to the first sacrifices they made.

"The code" that was to be solidified on the western frontier started developing with those first pilgrims.

The Journey There

The adventurous gene was passed down to the Ohio frontiersman's offspring. These young people didn't want to stay at home, where things were tame and boring. They wanted to go to the new frontier—the area called the Great Plains. So in the early 1840s, using Independence, Missouri, as the jumping-off point, these pioneers headed west. At the time, the area where they were heading was often called the great American desert.

To protect their possessions, they covered wagons with canvas stretched over wooden frames. As they traveled, one could look at them from a distance and imagine these wagons were ships crossing the plains. Thus, they acquired the name of "prairie schooners."

The bed or storage area of the wagon was about ten feet long and four feet wide. It's interesting to note that although the dimensions are different; this is about the same number of square feet as in today's California King Bed. Imagine putting everything you need for your future on your bed.

The animal of choice for pulling the covered wagons was mules. But there were few mules broke to the harness, and those that were, were expensive. Horses were great for riding but not pulling a wagon for months at a time. Most pioneers used two or three teams of oxen. Although they were slower than mules or horses, they were more dependable. Oxen could eat and survive on almost anything green. And Indians seldom stole oxen because they had no use for "cows." In addition, when the pioneer got to his final destination, the lowly ox provided a way to plow the field and even meat for the table.

Contrary to Hollywood movies, Indians rarely attacked wagon trains, either moving or at night. The number of people in a wagon train was too great. However, a lone wagon was easy to overcome. Incidentally, more pioneers were accidentally killed with their own firearms than were killed by Indians.

Even though these pioneers had high spirits and determination, none of the experiences in their past life could prepare them for the journey they were about to undertake. For safety reasons, families seldom, if ever, traveled alone. And sometimes, the wagon trains stretched as far as the eye could see. Traveling an average of fifteen miles a day, they were often short on water and food. Only the sick and the weak rode on the wagons.

The westward trail was not only strewn with some of the family's most-prized possessions, there were the carcasses of horses, mules, and oxen. With the ground often rock hard, human graves were shallow and unmarked to discourage grave robbers. Some estimates say there was an average of one grave every eighty yards. Unlike western movies, there was seldom music and dance in the evenings. Not only were the families dead tired, there were repairs to be made to the tack and the wagon. Quite often, it was raining, or the wind was blowing in a gale force. To survive, they had to literally "go the distance."

The Promised Land

Once the pioneer arrived at his destination, he was no longer an immigrant. He then became a settler.

When the frontier was in the East, a person's wealth was largely dependent on his willingness to work hard.

Land was basically free. To make it productive, it had to be cleared of trees and other vegetation. The size of his house was determined by the number of logs a person wanted to cut and stack on top of each other to make a cabin. For water, there was usually a stream close by. If not, it was just a matter of digging a well and have it fill up with water. Game was plentiful. And it was easy to stalk wild animals in the wooded areas.

When the plain's pioneers got to their destination, they looked around and saw no trees for building cabins. Basically, all the land had to offer was soil and grass. What were they to do? Creativity and ingenuity took hold.

"There is no shortcut to success: If you want to reach the Promised Land, you must go through the wilderness."

Initially, they used the covered wagon that brought them to the plains as their home. Then they took the canvas and wood from the wagon to construct tents. Some dug caves in the side of hills, facing away from the prevailing winds. They called these homes dugouts.

After they had taken care of their immediate needs, they noticed the plain's grasses grew so tight that it was almost impossible to turn the soil. So they decided to cut that soil into squares and stack the squares on top of each other, thus creating a sod home. It took about an acre of sod to construct an average-sized home.

Incidentally, as they were creating these sod squares, they realized the plow that had been used to turn over the eastern loamy soil just wouldn't work on the plains. So they came up with a heavier, sharper plow. Because the plow had two parallel iron rods that stuck up like an insect's wings, this plow got the nickname "grasshopper." And again using creativity, the ground that had been scalped to create the sod home was used as their garden.

That essential element, water, wasn't on the surface as it was in the East. They found it necessary to dig wells 150 or more feet deep. The sodbusters dug most of these wells by hand—one shovelful at a time. When the well got too deep to throw the dirt out of the hole, it was put in a bucket and pulled to the top. Once the well was dug, how did they get that water to the surface? Our frontiersmen came up with windmills. It has been said that covered wagons brought people to the plains, and windmills made it possible for them to stay there.

Life on the Plains

Building homes out of bricks of sod a foot wide by a foot-and-a-half long and about three inches thick wasn't easy. But like the log cabins of the East, the size of their home was determined by the amount of work they wanted to put into it and the number of friends who were willing to help them. What historians call the "principle of mutuality" or "being a good friend and neighbor" became a mainstay in frontier life.

The only real cost for a "soddy," as they came to be known, was the windows. The homes of poor settlers had fewer windows. The thick walls kept it cool in the summer and held in the heat during the winter. In addition, it was virtually fireproof. Some people "plastered" the interior walls with mud and painted them with whitewash.

However, more than humans occupied these homes. Insects of all kinds lived in the sod bricks. And larger animals, such as mice and snakes, lived in any crack they could find. There's even a story of a snake dropping from the roof onto the dinner table while the family was eating.

With a dirt floor, walls, and roof, the sod home was virtually impossible to keep clean. And when the thunderstorms of the plains came, the roof would leak muddy water. Even after the rains stopped outside, they continued for days on the inside. If the pioneer had them, everyone wore oilskin coats inside as well as outside. Mothers wrapped infants in oilcloths. The husband would hang a sheet over the stove to keep the mud out of the food during preparation. The earthen floor became mud, even though they had used a mixture of animal blood and salt to harden it.

In spite of it all, the pioneers were positive and cheerful. A poem found in an early journal expresses this:

> How happy I feel when I crawl into bed,
> And a rattlesnake rattles a tune at my head.
> And the gay little centipede void of all fear,
> Crawls over my neck and down into my ear.
> And the gay little bedbugs so cheerful and bright,
> Keep me a laughing two-thirds of the night.
> And the gay little flea with sharp tacks on his toes,
> Plays 'Why don't you catch me' all over my nose.

"Thanks. I think."

An essential item for every home was a stove. Often it was purchased before the pioneer started west. But almost any iron box could be used. With no trees for firewood, the pioneer started using small bundles of grass as fuel. But the grass would burn too fast and hot. Then they noticed the Plains Indians using dried "buffalo chips." It wasn't the ideal fuel. It was dirty and smelly. It burned hot and eventually ruined the stove. But it cooked food, warmed the home, and didn't cost anything.

A newspaper reporter observed women handled the buffalo chips gingerly at first. They started by picking them up with two sticks, then a rag, and then their apron. Finally, they picked them up with their hands and washed their hands afterward. He concluded by saying, "And now? Now it is out of the bread, into the chips, and back again—and not even a dust of the hands."

Life on the plains was sunup to sundown work for both the husband and the wife. This need for the woman to do much the same physical work as her husband elevated the woman's standing. Families tended to be large. Although children were loved as much or even more than today, at a young age, a child was put to work on the homestead. So the more children you had, the larger your "spread" could be.

Loneliness was rampant. More than one woman went mad. Even though they had neighbors, the neighbors were miles away. A trip to town or the nearest settler's store was an opportunity to talk to someone "from the outside." But it was usually the man who took the trip alone. Someone had to stay at home and tend the livestock and crops. And that person was the woman.

Because of this loneliness and confidence in the future, generosity came naturally for pioneers. Anyone who came by the homestead was invited in and asked to stay for a while. In turn, this hospitality wasn't taken lightly. The visitor would always offer to do some work around the place for his "keep."

Originally, towns comprising a few tents or false front buildings would start gathering around trading posts or army outposts. Often located along migration routes, the towns would be about twenty-five miles apart. This was the distance of a day's journey. It also meant farmers and ranchers were no more than a half-day's journey from supplies and a market.

"I prefer to look at it as a lifetime supply of fuel for the fire."

When the railroad came along, these towns would often pick up and move to a location close to the rails. Since the vast majority of the people occupying these areas were men, there were always more saloons than any other one business. It wasn't unusual for these saloons to also provide a restaurant, general store and hotel as well.

Towns often developed in a haphazard way, and businesses were on either side of a main street. Any private homes would be away from the business section. With no sewer system, wastewater was directed into small, open ditches or just "thrown outside." And this waste was often more than just dirty dishwater. Chickens and pigs were seldom confined by fences. Horses disposed of their "waste" at their leisure. It can be said with no fear of contradiction; living in or even visiting a town wasn't the healthiest thing to do.

If people did get sick, home remedies abounded. When someone was bitten by a snake, a poultice of warm manure was applied on the bitten area. Coal oil cured dandruff. And for measles, there was nothing better than a well-cooked mouse.

The Civil War and the Old West

While pioneers were fighting the elements in the West, a battle of another kind was developing in the East that would be almost as much of an influence on the future of the West as it was the East.

"It was also a war in which brother fought brother."

This was a war where neighbor fought neighbor; Missouri sent thirty-nine regiments to fight in the siege of Vicksburg. Seventeen of these regiments fought on the Confederate side, and twenty-two fought on the Union side. It was also a war in which brother fought brother. Senator John J. Crittendon of Kentucky had two sons, who were both major generals: one on the Union side and the other was a Confederate.

More than three million Americans fought in the Civil War, with 618,000 people killed. Obviously, the Civil War had a great influence on the direction and future of the Eastern United States. But not so obviously, the Civil War had almost as great an influence on the future of the West.

For soldiers returning home following the Civil War, what they had experienced during the war had matured them tremendously. Particularly in the south, often there were only ashes where the homestead was located four years before. In the north, where family homesteads still existed, these young men were no longer patient to spend years, working the farm before they were able to inherit it. In both cases, these young men looked to the West and the opportunities that lay there.

Texas came in on the side of the Confederacy. And the ranchers joined up, along with all able-bodied men. Even though the Confederacy was always in need of beef, the Union Navy blockaded the ports so no cattle could leave Texas. The young boys and old men left in charge of the Texas cattle weren't able to manage them.

When the cattlemen returned to their ranches, the cattle had multiplied like rabbits and were as wild as deer. The numbers of these wild animals were upward of five million. In addition, there was no local market. A cow was worth only a dollar or two, if the rancher could even find a buyer.

With the expansion of the frontier, Texas cattlemen looked to the north. In addition, the building of the transcontinental railroad provided other opportunities. At the same time, a young man by the name of Joseph McCoy conceived the idea of establishing a shipping point along the transcontinental railroad to transport live cattle to markets back east. Initially, he selected Abilene, Kansas. In Abilene, he built a Drover's Cottage, stockyards, and bank. Always a marketer, Joseph advertised throughout Texas, telling cattle ranchers of the opportunities up north. And they responded.

The young ex-soldiers who had come west were looking for work, and the cattlemen were looking for someone who was willing to work long hours at a dangerous job for little pay. Rounding up and driving cattle to a northern destination was a piece of cake when compared to being a soldier during the Civil War.

Unlike what is portrayed in the Hollywood movies, all cowboys weren't Anglo. Following the Civil War, approximately an eighth of the young men who came west to be cowboys were Black. There were also a number of Indian cowboys.

With the exception of a few die-hard ex-Confederates, there was little discrimination, especially on the trail. Like the frontier throughout America's history, a person's origins, his titles, or his past meant little. A man was accepted or rejected based on the level of his contribution, not where he came from. And the concept of respecting the other person was strengthened.

> "The concept of respecting the other person was strengthened."

These weren't the first "cowboys." For generations, the Spanish had worked with cattle. These vaqueros developed the equipment and the techniques to control what some early cowboys called the dumbest beast on God's earth.

The young cowboys were fast learners. They observed the vaqueros and were quick to pick up their techniques. Unfortunately, in the translation of words and actions, many subtleties were lost. *La reata* became *lariat*; *Chaparreras* was shortened to *chaps*; a *mestano* turned into a *mustang*; the dreaded *estampida* was now a *stampede*; *vaqueros* were *buckaroos*; and somehow *cabellerango* became *wrangler*.

The cowboy who came from the East looked at how the vaquero handled his horse and the cattle and was able to accomplish the same end but not always using the same technique. The vaquero had spent a lifetime learning on how to train and ride a horse. Although the cowboy could "ride anything with hair," he didn't have the patience of the vaquero. His method of training a horse was to "buck him out," and he depended on the horses' natural skills rather than spending time in training and developing a relationship as the vaquero did. The cowboy may not have been subtle. For sure, he wasn't a quitter.

Origins of the Cowboy

There are several stories about the origins of the word *cowboy*. One is that the term started in England and Scotland where young boys tended the cows. Another is that in New England colonial days, there were gangs of young men who stole cattle. These men were called cowboys. Still another is that it came from the south where young Black slaves took care of the plantation's cattle.

Originally, it was two words. In the early 1800s, it was a hyphenated word, cow-boy. Then, as time progressed, it became one word.

In the Wild Old West, many an outlaw or gang were called cowboys. In addition, young men from sixteen years of age to their mid-twenties, who worked on ranches doing an honest day's work, were also called cowboys. One reporter felt cowpunchers were honest men simply because they never insulted a woman.

For our purposes, we're going to focus on the young cowboys doing an honest day's work.

Cow Hunts

Following the Civil War, with some five million cows running wild in southeast Texas below the Nueces River, young men looking for a job, and the prospects of a market for the cattle "up north," the Texas ranchers put together what they called cow hunts. The cowboys would go into the brush and forested areas to hunt out these "beeves," which were often called mossy horns because some of them actually had been in the woods so long that they had moss on their horns.

After the cattle were rounded up, a neutral person, who was commonly agreed on, would check to see if there were any remnants of a brand. If so, that cow and any calf with it belonged to the brand's ranch. Those cattle with no brand were divided up equitably or gambled for on a hand of poker. This was all done in a friendly and neighborly way, and each rancher trusted the other to be fair. And just like companies today, the moral standards of that company were established by the management. So the cowboys, following management's standards, also practiced fairness in their personal dealings.

After the spring roundup, a large ranch, or several small ranches, would organize a cattle drive to a railhead like Abilene, Kansas.

Life on the Trail

As indicated earlier, even the harshest experience out west was nothing compared to what many of the young men experienced during the Civil War. Watching western movies about cattle drives are deceptive, and they leave a lot out.

The day began at 4:00 a.m. with breakfast. The cook had gotten up at 3:00 a.m. After breakfast, each cowboy caught and saddled his own horse. Prior to leaving Texas, each cowboy had chosen six to eight horses that were his to ride during the trail drive. A cowboy never rode someone else's horse.

At daylight, the cattle were moved off their bed and allowed to graze for a while. With the men taking their assigned places as point, swing, flank, or drag, the cattle were pushed out. Incidentally, drag, the dirtiest job was given to the tenderfeet.

The cook and the chuck wagon had gone ahead of the herd to select a place for the noon meal called dinner. After dinner, the cowboys got fresh horses. The cook, extra horses, and cowboys standing first watch went ahead to find a night camp.

At the end of the day, the cattle were allowed to graze before being put to bed. The cowboys had another meal and went to bed.

There were strict rules. Along with saddling and riding your own horse, no one complained about the long hours, hard work, or food. A complainer was a shirker. So whether or not they were happy about their working conditions, everyone was, at least outwardly, positive and cheerful.

"Only quitters complain, and cowboys hate quitters."

The cook's area was off limits to be entered only when invited. To get on the good side of the cook, cowboys would bring in wood for the cook fire. When it was time to change the watch at night, a cowboy was always awakened by voice, never touch. Anyone who didn't follow the rules or was a troublemaker became an outcast, who was simply ignored by the others.

Incidentally, at night, the cook always pointed the tongue of the chuck wagon toward the North Star. That way, no matter what the weather conditions the next morning, they knew the direction to go.

This routine was interrupted only during times of sheer terror. Stampedes were the greatest fear. Some cattle herds seemed to stampede at every opportunity. Rivers were another problem. Most cowboys didn't know how to swim. Sometimes when cattle crossed a river, the lead steers would get to the midpoint and then turn back. This would start the cattle milling in a circle in the middle of the river. The unlucky cowboys had to go into the cattle and get them going in the correct direction. Incidentally, more cowboys drowned crossing rivers than were killed by Indians.

Then there were the human problems. There were the Kansas Jayhawkers, Red Legs, and Bushwhackers, who demanded money or cattle. Indians weren't normally this direct. They would simply start a stampede at night and pick up some of the strays.

Remembering these cowboys were teenagers or in their early twenties and remembering how we were at that age, it's amazing how responsible these young men were. There was a term they used—ride for the brand—which meant they had loyalty to the ranch, people working for that ranch, and any cow with the ranch's brand on it to the point that they were willing to give their lives for that brand. This is because when they started working for the ranch, they had given their word to do so.

Traveling at twelve to fifteen miles a day, the drive went on for about two months. Then they arrived at their destination in Kansas.

The Cattle Town

In order to receive the cattle being brought up from Texas, cattle towns sprang up in Kansas as the transcontinental railroad headed west. They included Abilene, Caldwell, Dodge City, Ellsworth, Newton, and Wichita.

The towns had two main purposes: to put cattlemen and buyers together and to show the cowboys the "elephant," a term that meant seeing the bright lights and excitement of the city.

Cattle towns were wild and woolly. Once the herd was sold and the cowboys paid, typically a cowboy wanted a hot bath and a new set of clothes. He had probably been wearing the same outfit since he left Texas. Then came a great meal. For whatever the reason, fresh oysters and eggs were a favorite. They sure weren't interested in a steak.

We've all seen movies and read novels about the actions of wild cowboys in cattle towns. First, all cowboys weren't wild. Many a cowboy went into town, got cleaned up, had a good meal, and returned to camp ready for the ride back home. And he still had money in his pocket. These were the young men who became cattlemen or businessmen themselves. But there were others who, as one cowboy said, "I had to sow my wild oats, and I regret to say that I also sowed all my money right along with the oats."

There are as many contemporary accounts of cattle-drive cowboys being people of character as there are accounts of them being ruffians. We must remember these were young people in their teens and early twenties, who had just spent two months doing an almost impossible job.

As we mentioned earlier, there is a good illustration of something similar today—college students on spring break. Most students spend spring break quietly at home. However, if one goes by the news they read and hear, one may think wild parties and drunken binges were what every college student did during spring break.

End of an Era

Although most historians don't end the Old West until the first part of the twentieth century, according to the census bureau's definition of a settled land—two or more persons per square mile—the United States was settled by 1890.

Men were alive when Lewis and Clark first explored the West, who were alive when the West was no longer classified as a frontier. It happened in that short of a time.

The heyday of a cowboy, called the Wild West, was much shorter, only about twenty years from the end of the Civil War to the mid-1880s. Cattle drives were no longer necessary; the railroad had come to Texas. In addition, thousands of miles of barbed wire had fenced in the cattle. Those cowboys who still had a job became ranch hands, fixing fences. Even the ranch atmosphere had changed. Where originally the ranch owner had worked, eaten, and slept alongside his hands, now most ranches were owned by eastern or European companies, with rules being established that were foreign to the cowboys.

The Code

What began back in the 1620s with the arrival of the Puritans, their work ethic, and a realization of the need for cooperation for survival continued, as pioneers went west with barn raisings, fair play, and loyalty.

When the cowboys came along, these young men shared the hardships and dangers of roundups and cattle drives, as well as the loneliness of line shacks during the winter. This resulted in a special camaraderie and a society based on trust and dependence. These cowboys started formalizing these precepts, even on occasion writing some of them down.

Our belief is that observing these precepts has made us the great nation we are today. In addition, the continued observation of these precepts will serve us well. Wouldn't you love to have friends who live their lives in accordance to these seven precepts?

It's one thing to determine to follow the precepts. But just what does "respect yourself and others" mean? Does being fair in all my dealings mean I should allow people to take advantage of me?

What follows is an interpretation of what it means to put these seven principles into practice.

If I say something, that you may think is out in left field: don't reject everything else. Someone else might just find it valuable. On the other hand, that "someone else" might think the gem you just read is for the birds. This book is a bit like a good bowl of vegetable soup. Try it; it can't hurt.

Chapter 3

Respect Yourself and Others

The Importance of Respecting Yourself

As the story goes, the Queen of England's yacht was traveling strange waters at night. The yacht's lookout saw a bright light coming directly at them. He notified the captain. The yacht's captain told the signalman to signal the oncoming ship to alter its course. The signal came back. "You alter your course."

Angrily, the queen's captain told the signalman to send, "This is the captain of the Queen's yacht. You alter your course."

The signal came back, "This is the keeper of the lighthouse. You alter your course."

It's not by accident that the first two words of "the code" are "respect yourself." These are without a doubt the most important words of the code. "Respecting yourself" is essential if one is to have the ability to observe the other precepts. Our ability to like other people is controlled by our ability to like ourselves. Our ability to accept other people is limited by our ability to accept ourselves. Possibly, by the end of this chapter, you will understand that a course change may be necessary in your life.

Each time I read this first precept, I'm reminded of the 1968 Aretha Franklin song that starts "R-E-S-P-E-C-T find out what it means to me."

Unfortunately, quite often, respecting ourselves is one of the most difficult things we have to do in life. We know our darkest secrets, and that's scary. Our failures loom in front of us like giant elephants. And I know, at least for me, these elephants have the ability to block out the future.

A hundred people can say we're good at something, but let one person criticize us, and we feel, "Finally, someone has been honest with me." That's in part because it has been estimated that for every positive stimulus we receive, there are ten negative ones. If we had encountered this level of support when, as an infant, we were learning to walk, we would probably all be crawling to this day.

So in reality, one can understand why people lack self-respect and, at the same time, marvel that there are those who live lives of self-confidence. Making mistakes and being imperfect is a part of life. There has been but one person who was perfect, and He ended up being turned in by one of his closest friends and hanged from a cross.

We need to enjoy our successes and learn from our failures. At one point, while trying to come up with the light bulb, Thomas Edison said, "I have not failed. I've just found 10,000 ways that won't work."

> "It's impossible to fail. If you do something that doesn't work, you've just found another way not to do it."

We're not going to spend time analyzing why we may lack self-respect. That ends up in our playing the blame game. And to blame circumstances or other people for our condition gives the circumstances or other people all the power. To live a life of confidence requires all the power we can muster.

Change Is Essential

If we don't have self-confidence and want to have it, it's essential that we make major changes in our lives. Craziness has been defined as doing the same thing over and over and expecting different results.

Porsche Nelson wrote the following:

Autobiography in Five Short Chapters

Chapter one: I walk down the street. There's a deep hole in the sidewalk. I fall in. I'm helpless. It's not my fault. It takes forever to find my way out.

Chapter two: I walk down the same street. There's a deep hole in the sidewalk. I fall in again. I can't believe I'm in the same place. But it isn't my fault. It still takes a long time to get out.

Chapter three: I walk down the same street. There's a deep hole in the sidewalk. I see it's there. I still fall in. It's a habit. My eyes are open. I know where I am. It's my fault. I get out immediately.

Chapter four: I walk down the same street. There's a deep hole in the sidewalk. I see it's there. I walk around it.

Chapter five: I walk down another street.

People who are addicted to drugs or alcohol often find just knowing there's a deep hole in the street where they walk isn't enough. They have to walk down another street. What follows is an outline on how to "walk down another street."

Ten Steps in Gaining Self-confidence

"It may be that your sole purpose in life is to be kind to others."

Words and thoughts are like seeds. Every time we say something negative or have a negative or destructive thought, we're planting a seed. The ground where these seeds are planted is extremely fertile, and that seed will sprout and take a life of its own, producing fruit. Below are ten steps we can take to make sure the seeds we plant are positive and producing victory and success.

1. Don't Put Limits on Yourself

We all remember hearing and even repeating to our children that childhood story about the little engine who, after larger engines were asked and refused, agreed to pull a train up a grade. Even though everyone thought it impossible, the little engine hooked on to the train and repeating, "I think I can," pulled the train up the grade.

The other day, my wife, Sunny, was in the middle of fixing dinner, and she asked me to get her a stick of butter from the refrigerator. Normally, I'm more than willing to help her. But I was watching "Law & Order" on TV, and it was time for the bad guy to confess.

So reluctantly, I got up and headed for the kitchen. On the way to the refrigerator, I said to myself, "I can't find anything in there. It's always packed with jars, containers, and stuff."

After two minutes of moving containers of leftover food—some with a science project going on inside—I said, "I can't find the butter. It's not in here."

Sunny walked over and grabbed the butter from the shelf right in front of me. Of course, she had to remark, "If it had been a snake, it would have bitten you."

I had just experienced what psychologists call a self-fulfilling prophesy. When I said, "I can't find anything in the refrigerator," I gave my brain the command not to find the butter.

Because our brain does whatever it's commanded to do, although my eyes saw the butter, my brain refused to acknowledge its presence.

It's been said, "Whether you believe you can or can't do something, you're right." And this was a perfect example. In addition, when we say we can't do something, we usually don't even try. And if we do make an attempt, we sure don't want to prove ourselves wrong. So we don't put in the effort. Then we can say to everyone, "See, I told you so."

A philosophical question: If a person says he'll fail and he fails, has he actually succeeded?

The expectation one has is extremely powerful. A number of years ago, Dr. Robert Rosenthal of Harvard University did an experiment in the San Francisco school system. Three teachers were told they would each be teaching a class of exceptional students.

The teachers were asked not to inform the students or their parents about the uniqueness of the classes. At the end of the experiment, the students not only got the highest grades in their school, they also got the highest in their district.

The teachers were then told their students weren't exceptional. The students had been selected at random. The teachers responded by indicating that obviously the students succeeded because the district's top three teachers taught them. "Not so," said Dr. Rosenthal, "the three of you were also selected at random."

This is the law of expectation. We get those results we expect. How can we get the good things in life when we're convinced that they aren't for us and that we're not deserving of them? We tend to get what we expect and feel we deserve.

Too often, we work for one thing yet expect something much less. All this does is put a governor on our actions. We don't go into the ring prepared to win. No matter what we thought of boxer Mohamed Ali, everyone knew when he stepped into the ring; he expected to win and had "laid it on the line."

We have all read at least one story of how a slightly build person was able to lift an automobile that had fallen on a loved one. When that person is interviewed afterward, he usually responded by saying he didn't even ask himself if he could or couldn't do it. He just did it.

Sure, this miraculous event happened under special circumstances. But each of our lives is miraculous. We are all special. There is no one else like us. And whether we want to accept it or not, each of us is roaming this earth for a purpose. That purpose may be great such as discovering the cure for cancer, or it may be as simple as being an inspiration to others with similar handicaps and limitations. So it's essential that we don't put limitations on ourselves.

Whether it's a habit or addiction that is keeping us from respecting ourselves, God has given each of us the power to overcome. Remember to always tell yourself you are not going to overcome or trying to overcome, but you are overcoming.

Don't be constantly thinking about your problems. Our thoughts create the environment in which we live. Focusing always on our problems creates an atmosphere of perpetual defeat.

Instead of thinking about your problems, think about the solution to your problems. That puts you mentally and emotionally on the right track. As Joel Osteen says, "Quit speaking words of defeat, and start speaking words of victory. Don't use your words to describe your situation; use your words to change your situation."

2. Forgive Yourself

Forgive yourself? That's right, forgive yourself. Our ministers and the Bible are always encouraging us to forgive people who offend us. Even the people who offend us regularly ask our forgiveness. Moreover, our ministers, the Bible, as well as the offenders are correct. We must forgive others.

> "You don't have to wait for someone to bring you flowers. Plant your own garden."

There is another element of forgiveness that we seldom think about; that's forgiving ourselves. How often have we said to ourselves, "I'll never forgive myself for doing or saying that." Or we beat ourselves up because of something stupid we said or did. If we can be gracious enough to forgive others, why can't we forgive ourselves?

"A forgiven person has no past. An unforgiven person has no future." This statement has implications beyond the forgiveness given by God. It also refers to the forgiveness a person gives himself. If you can't forgive yourself for errors of the past—even those things that were just plain bad—your focus will always be on the past. You will spend your time kicking yourself for things you can't change and living in the fear that you will repeat them.

It was the bottom of the ninth inning in a crucial baseball game. The score was tied. The coach called time out and walked to the mound. He told the pitcher; "This batter likes the ball low and outside. So don't pitch it low and outside." As he was walking back to the dugout, he again said, "Don't pitch low and outside." The umpire called "play ball". The batter stepped into the box. The pitcher went into the windup and threw the ball low and outside. The batter hit a home run. After the game, the pitcher said, "Why did the coach keep saying 'low and outside'? Even though he said not to pitch the ball to that spot, all I could think was low and outside, and that's the very place where I pitched it."

If you forgive yourself, you can concentrate on the present and look forward to the future. By focusing on your past, those things will be more likely to repeat themselves. Because that which we focus our mind on tends to become reality.

Research shows that the physical and the psychological reactions to not being able to forgive and forget cause blood to clot more quickly and inhibit digestion, and it can even be a major contribution to a stroke or heart attack.

According to the *Journal of Personality and Social Psychology*, a person's attitude toward themselves could even affect their immune system. The report shows that the levels of T-cells, a measure of immunity, rose by 13 percent when people who were optimistic about themselves faced a challenge but dropped by 3 percent when people who were pessimistic about themselves faced the same challenge.

3. List Your Strengths

Believe it or not, everyone has his or her strengths. Even the two of us. And if you're honest and objective with yourself, you'll find you have a lot more than you thought. Sometimes what initially you may think is a weakness may very well be turned into a strength.

When Picasso was in grade school, he was terrible in math. It wasn't that he was dumb. It was that he always got detracted. Each time he wrote a number such as 4, he would see a face in the number, and it became the beginning of a drawing. Thankfully, his teacher didn't go about destroying this strength.

Here is a parable that illustrates this principle beautifully:

An elderly Chinese woman had two large pots, which hung on the ends of a pole that she carried across her neck.

One of the pots had a crack in it. At the end of the long walks from the stream to the house, the cracked pot arrived only half full. The other pot delivered a full portion of water.

Each day for two years, the woman brought home only one-and-a-half pots of water.

Of course, the perfect pot was proud of what it was able to accomplish.

But the poor cracked pot was ashamed of its imperfection and miserable that it could only do half of what it had been made to do.

After two years of being a failure, the broken pot spoke to the woman, "I'm ashamed of myself. This crack in my side causes water to leak out all the way back to your house."

The old woman smiled. "Did you notice that there are flowers on your side of the path but not on the other pot's side? That's because I have always known about your flaw, so I planted flower seeds on your side of the path, and every day while we walk back, you water the flowers.

"I have been able to pick these beautiful flowers to decorate the table. Without you being just the way you are, there would not be this beauty to grace the house."

Even being a crackpot can sometimes be a strength.

"Everyone has strengths."

4. Take Responsibility for Yourself

We're not going to spend much time on this step because the whole next chapter will be on accepting responsibility.

Recently, a trial was concluded for two men who committed a home invasion in which three members of a family were brutally killed. The first person's defense was that it wasn't his fault. His lawyers maintained that if the police had gotten there sooner, they would have prevented him from committing that atrocious crime. So the police should be on trial, not him. When the second person went on trial, the defense blamed the victims because they didn't try hard enough to get away. This may sound extreme, but sometimes our excuses are just as bad.

If it's not parents, drugs, or DNA, it's just the way I was made, and there's nothing I can do about it. It seems everyone has an excuse for everything.

If you haven't already realized it, none of us is perfect, either physically or emotionally. Everyone has aspects about their life they don't particularly like. My belief is we're made imperfect in order for us to develop the character to overcome these imperfections, not to fall victim to them.

The bottom line is if we say we're a certain way because people or circumstances have made us that way, we've given those people or circumstances the responsibility and the power over our condition, and we put our life under the control of others. The willingness to accept responsibility for one's own life is the source from which respect for yourself originates. It also lets us maintain the power necessary to make the changes to correct that condition.

If you need more encouragement to take responsibility for your life, jump ahead to Chapter 3. But do remember to come back to this chapter. There's some great stuff coming up.

5. Surround Yourself with Quality People

My father used to tell me, "You're known by the company you keep." And chances are, if it wasn't your father, someone who loved you probably told you something similar.

I don't know about your loved one, but my father didn't want me to associate with young people who would hang around a coffee shop called the Dew Drop Inn. These were guys who smoked and drank and dated women who did the same. Incidentally, this took place during a different age and time.

I'm not talking about the "Dew Droppers" as we called them back then. What I'm talking about is surrounding yourself with people of quality.

Too often, we like to have a lot of friends because it makes us feel popular. But often these are not really friends. At best, they're merely acquaintances.

Just because a person is a friend doesn't mean that that person is a "good" friend. If your friend brings you down or shows you disrespect, it's time for a reevaluation. It's not healthy to have friends who are constantly putting you and themselves down. What I'm talking about is not good-natured give-and-take ribbing. A good friend is someone who is constantly challenging you to be a better person, not necessarily by words but by their example.

Friends accept us the way we are, warts and all. If you find yourself becoming a chameleon in order to please your friends, there's a problem in the relationship. You need to be able to be yourself. If you aren't true to your core values, I can assure you your friends will know it, and they won't respect you.

If you have friends who are positive and cheerful, are fair in their dealings, are people of their word, and are willing to go the distance, then you are one of the lucky few.

We'll talk more about friends in Chapter 8.

6. Have Confidence in Yourself

We think of people who are shy and insecure as people with a low self-esteem, and therefore they never think about themselves. On the other hand, we classify people as conceited when they think of no one but themselves.

Using this standard, quite possibly, the insecure person is just as conceited as the loudmouth, who tells everyone how great he is. The insecure person is always focused on what people think of them. They're always thinking about how they should act in each situation they encounter. In effect, they're always thinking about themselves. The only real difference between them and the people we normally classify as conceited is insecure people aren't honest enough to tell us that they're stuck on themselves.

Admittedly, if one has confidence in themselves, it very well could be interpreted by some as conceit. In reality, we do almost everything because we're conceited enough to believe we can do it. Getting in our automobile and driving at sixty-five miles an hour on a two-lane highway takes a lot of confidence in our skills.

> "Don't let anybody's opinion kill your belief in yourself."

Self-confidence has overcome more obstacles and difficulties than any other human quality.

Before Theodore Roosevelt became the president of the United States, he was a cowboy and rancher. As a boy, Roosevelt was sickly and fearful. Later in life, he wrote the following:

"When a boy, I read a passage in one of Marryat's books, which always impressed me. In this passage, the captain of some small British man-of-war is explaining to the hero how to acquire the quality of fearlessness. He says that at the outset almost every man is frightened when he goes into action, but that the course to follow is for the man to keep such a grip on himself that he can act just as if he were not frightened. After this is kept up long enough, it changes from pretense to reality, and the man does in very fact become fearless by sheer dint of practicing fearlessness when he does not feel it.

"This was the theory upon which I went. There were all kinds of things of which I was afraid at first, ranging from grizzly bears to 'mean' horses and gunfighters; but by acting as if I was not afraid, I gradually ceased to be afraid. Most men can have the same experience if they choose."

Theodore Roosevelt's experience should teach us a couple of lessons about self-confidence. The first is that just because a person is self-confident, doesn't mean he's fearless. A self-confident person can be just as afraid as the rest of us. The difference is that they "act" self-confident. The second is that by acting self-confident, a person actually becomes self-confident.

But there are some areas where just "acting" isn't enough. In order to support those actions, there has to be a level of knowledge.

"I am not afraid.
I am not afraid.
I am not afraid.
  I am not....."

In what area would you like to become more self-confident? If you would just take thirty minutes each day to read books and articles and talk to experts about this subject, in one year, you would have spent over 180 hours educating yourself, and in a short time, you would have a virtual doctor's degree on that subject. And for sure, you would be more knowledgeable in this area than almost everyone else on this planet. But watch out. With all that knowledge and power, you could become a human dynamo and go on to do and create outstanding things.

7. Carry Yourself with Confidence

I'm six foot five inches tall. As long as I can remember, I've been taller than my peers. And like most young people, I really didn't like standing out in the crowd. So I would droop my shoulders and stand in a way that would make me look shorter. Although I didn't realize it at the time, I had wise parents. They would say, "Stand up straight. Be proud of your height." To get them off my back, I would stand up straight. What I didn't realize at the time, my standing up straight gave me an air of confidence that I really didn't have. And as a result, people treated me with respect, even though I was just a dumb kid.

Having a lack of confidence is not only a mental state; it's also a physical one. Dr. Paul Ekman, professor of psychiatry at the University of California in San Francisco said, "We know that if you have an emotion, it shows on our face. Now we've seen it goes the other way too. We become what we put on our face. If we laugh at suffering, we don't feel suffering inside. If our face shows sorrow, we do feel it inside." Professor Ekman maintains that people regularly beat lie detectors by putting themselves in a physiology of belief.

Notice the people around you. Their bodies reflect their emotion. Frown, drooped shoulders, a lowered head, and a shuffling walk show one thing—depression. It's not an easy state to get into. Depressed people have to work at it.

The police tell us muggers look for someone who is walking at a slow pace with head down as if they have no purpose in what they're doing. It show muggers they are not aware of their surroundings, and they're easily victimized.

People with confidence walk quickly. These people give the impression they have places to go, people to see, and important work to do. Muggers stay away from these people because they will fight back. So I guess a by-product of carrying ourselves with confidence is we won't get mugged as much.

> "If it's going to be,
>
> it's up to me."

By practicing good posture, we'll automatically feel a higher level of confidence. If we stand up straight, keep our head up, and make eye contact, we'll make a positive impression on others and instantly feel more alert and empowered.

If we go about with the feeling of inferiority in our face and manner, if everything about us indicates that we don't believe in ourselves, and we don't respect ourselves, we can't blame other people for not taking us at our word.

Try an experiment. Stand tall; throw your shoulders back; lift your head; put a smile on your face; breathe deeply; and put a spring in your step. You can't be depressed in that state.

8. Don't Abuse Yourself

The way a person treats himself or herself shows the respect they have for themselves. At this point, I may be considered doing some moralizing, as if much of or this entire book doesn't fall into that category.

A few years back, before we had cell phones, I traveled a lot, often along rural highways. So for safety, I got a CB radio for my truck. One day, while traveling down a two-lane country road, I overheard two truckers talking to each other. The conversation got on their aches and pains. One trucker said to the other, "If I'd known I would live this long, I would have taken better care of myself."

People who drink or smoke excessively and people who overeat, never exercise, and burn the candle at both ends, whether they want to accept it or not, show other people that they don't respect themselves. In addition, they sap their energy for achieving excellence.

It has been said that fatigue makes cowards of us all. Maybe we can't have the body of an athlete, but we can make every effort to keep our body in good working order. Until medicine becomes much more advanced than it presently is, this is the only body we have. We should treat it at least as well as we treat our automobile or other adult toys. By eating right, exercising, and practicing healthy habits, we'll not only feel better, we feel a sense of pride. This should be done, not because we don't like the way we are, but because it makes us feel better.

> "Fix the problem, not the blame."

A country preacher was delivering a great sermon. The "amen corner" was regularly shouting their encouragement. Then the minister started talking about specific sins. The amen corner was quiet. Concerned, the minister asked the problem. One of the deacons said, "Reverend, you've done stopped preaching and gone to meddling."

It's time to meddle. There is another area where we Americans tend to abuse ourselves, not in a direct way, but it affects us physically as much as any of the others we mentioned. That is our finances.

We're all like the child in the toy store screaming, "I want it now!" Newly married young people feel they need a place like their parent's home, not realizing it took their parents thirty years to work up to that home. We want a bigger car than our neighbor's, not knowing it's leased and he's two months behind in payments.

When we have a negative balance in our checking account, penalties and interest are taking the balance on our credit cards out of sight, and we're getting phone calls requesting past-due payments, both emotionally and physically, we're abusing our bodies more than if we went on a four-day drunk.

Even though the situation may seem hopeless, and we may want to crawl under our bed and never come out, this is not the time to go into a catatonic state of inaction. We need to call our creditors and the bank. Be honest with them. It's amazing how terrible situations don't seem as bad when we face them.

We also need to sit down with our family and develop a plan to make drastic cutbacks in our spending. It may be necessary to live on baloney for a while, instead of prime rib. We may have to visit Goodwill instead of Nordstroms. Incidentally, Goodwill has some great finds. Just ask my wife.

We can all be assured that facing the problem and solving it is nowhere as terrible as we imagine in our head.

9. Don't Let Other People's Emotions Control Your Emotions

Have you ever been driving down the highway on a beautiful morning with the feeling that you could take on any problem? Then someone you had unknowingly offended pulled beside you. That person proceeded to inform you of your mother's occupation, your heritage, and that you're number one. As a result, you're in a funk for the rest of the day.

That person probably had an argument with his wife that morning about a past-due house payment. In addition, he was going to be late for work, again. He was actually expressing to you the anger he felt about the conditions in his life.

Even if you didn't respond to him in a like manner, in a period of just five seconds, you let a total stranger control your emotions by allowing him to ruin your morning. Don't give strangers this power.

There will always be people who spend their life pulling others down to where they are. It's their way of maintaining control. And the more we try to please them, the more they will twist us into a pretzel.

A father and his son decided to take their donkey to an auction. Since they lived a short distance from the auction yard, and rather than trailer the donkey over, they decided to walk it there. They hadn't gotten very far when someone walked up and criticized the father for not adequately utilizing the carrying capacity of the donkey. So he put his son on the donkey.

Then they encountered another person who chastised the son for riding when his elderly father walked. So the father and his son exchanged places.

Another person later said it wasn't proper etiquette for a son to walk behind his father like a servant. So they both got on the donkey.

Next, they were criticized for overloading the donkey.

In frustration, the father tied the four feet of the donkey together and stuck a pole between them, and he and his son carried the donkey on their shoulders.

I swear there are people who, if they were given a million dollars in one-hundred dollar bills, would respond by saying, "But these are one-hundred dollar bills. Do you have any idea how hard they are to cash?" There's a saying that goes something like this: "You would complain even if you were hanged with a new rope."

Thank goodness that everyone doesn't believe what people say to them.

Thomas Edison's teachers said he was too stupid to learn anything. Beethoven's teacher once told him that he was hopeless as a composer. The famous opera singer Enrico Caruso's parents wanted him to be an engineer, and his teachers said he couldn't sing. Walt Disney was fired from a newspaper because the editor said he lacked ideas. Albert Einstein didn't speak until he was four and didn't read until he was seven. His teacher described him as "mentally slow, unsociable and adrift forever in his foolish dreams." Vince Lombardi, the great professional football coach known for his ability to motivate his players, early in his coaching career had an expert say of him, "He possesses minimal football knowledge. Lacks motivation."

Aren't we all glad these people didn't accept what was said about them? There would be no electric light bulbs. Classical music would be sadly lacking. We wouldn't be able to talk about the theory of relativity. And worst of all, there would be no Disneyland to go to escape reality.

What about you? Do you believe the bad things people say about you or do you believe in yourself?

Marianne Williamson in *A Return to Love* wrote, "Our deepest fear is not that we are inadequate. Our deepest fear is that we are powerful beyond measure. It is our light, not our darkness, that most frightens us. We ask ourselves, 'Who am I to be brilliant, gorgeous, talented, fabulous?' Actually, who are you not to be? You are a child of God. Your playing small doesn't serve the world. There's nothing enlightening about shrinking so that other people won't feel insecure around you. We are all meant to shine, as children do. We were born to make manifest the glory of God that is within us. It's not just in some of us; it's in everyone. And as we let our own light shine, we unconsciously give other people permission to do the same. As we're liberated from our own fear, our presence automatically liberates others."

10. Treat Others with Respect

Treating others with respect will also develop respect for yourself. People who treat others with disrespect often do so because they lack respect for themselves.

Treating others with respect will encourage them to treat you the same way.

This leads us to the second half of the first precept—respect others.

Respect Others

Respect is without a doubt the most important element in a successful long-term relationship. Let's start with the basics.

1. Basic Manners

A while back, I attended a concert given by my friend, cowboy singer R. W. Hampton. Following the concert, a young man about fifteen years of age came up to R. W. to tell him how much he enjoyed his music. During the conversation, the young man repeatedly said "sir" and "Mr. Hampton."

Afterward, R. W. came up to me and said, "That's something you don't see very often anymore—respect." Incidentally, the young man lived on a ranch and was being home schooled.

These are the manners of another time. It's what was taught back during the days of Ozzie and Harriet. Today, people—both young and old—are losing common courtesy. "Please," "thank you," and "excuse me" aren't heard as often as they should be heard. When someone says "sir," it's a good bet that that person had recently spent time in the military.

As a kid, I can remember being spanked. Yes, I was spanked because I didn't show proper respect to an adult. I can assure you I never made that mistake again.

There's a core of TV shows and movies that celebrate being rude and disrespectful. Amazingly, they seem to be popular. With these examples, one can understand why young people and adults feel it's the "in thing" to be crude. In addition, with our electronic age of e-mails and texting, we typically go for brevity. And that brevity doesn't allow for the expression of common courtesies.

The practice of basic manners benefits both the person showing the manners and the person receiving the respect.

Lest anyone thinks I'm speaking entirely about young people, adults can be just as bad.

But what about those times when someone shows us disrespect. Can we return it to them in like kind?

The story is told of Buddha being approached by a stranger with the objective of provoking Buddha into becoming angry. After the stranger had spent several minutes piling vindictiveness against Buddha, in a calm tone Buddha said, "Let me ask you a question. When a person is offered a gift, and he chooses not to receive it, to whom does it belong?"

"It remains the possession of the person offering the gift," replied the stranger.

Buddha then said, "I choose not to accept your anger. Therefore, it belongs to you."

Try never to return a lack of courtesy. But in every opportunity possible, show people common courtesies. If nothing else, it will confuse them.

"Try never to return a lack of courtesy."

2. Don't Prejudge

I can't count the number of times during my lifetime I have prejudged someone because of things like the frown on their face or the clothes they were wearing, only to find out they were experiencing a difficult time or they had just been working on a plumbing emergency under their house and hadn't had a chance to clean up.

One of my pet peeves is someone not returning my phone call. An incident that took place a couple of years ago taught me to watch my prejudgments.

After making several phone calls to a prospective supplier and not getting a return call, I finally got him on the line. Doing little to disguise my anger, I told the person that I had been trying to call him for two weeks. He told me he was sorry he didn't get back to me, but he had been in the hospital. Of course, anger was immediately replaced with embarrassment. After expressing my sorrow for his being in the hospital, I asked him what was wrong. He said, "I was giving a kidney to a friend." You can only imagine how low I felt. The lesson was learned.

It's not just lowly people such as me who prejudge. Even President Obama can be caught up in it. And he had to correct the prejudgment with a "beer summit."

I'm sure we all realize the area where prejudgment seems to occur most often involves race. The United States is not unique in this area. Virtually, every country on this great planet has had similar problems. Sometimes, it's based on color, other times tribe, and still others economics.

We've all heard or read that portion of Martin Luther King's "I Have a Dream" speech where he says he has a dream that one day he will live in a nation where people will not be judged by the color of their skin but by the content of their character.

I truly believe we're getting closer to that great day Dr. King dreamed about. But there are those who are keeping us away from it.

Prior to the 1960s, one could find a way to rationalize the feeling of inferiority toward people of another race or color. In many areas, there were prejudices commonly accepted both socially and legally. But today with a new understanding of God's creating all people equal and people of all colors accomplishing great things, there is absolutely no excuse for people showing prejudice to others, even of our own color, whatever that may be.

I'm afraid once again, as the deacon said, I'm going to stop preaching and start meddling. I also have to acknowledge there are those people on the other side of the spectrum who are also perpetuating this same prejudging by constantly playing "the race card." They not only point out legitimate racial actions but often interpret others' words and actions as racial "code words or actions," even adding "imagined" racial words to a person's comments.

We need to examine the motives of these people just as the people we typically call "racists" because quite often, their motivation isn't pure. Many times, they're not promoting racial equality but a political position or their own job security.

When we encounter people on either side of the spectrum, who are promoting racial tension, we need to tell them that we don't subscribe to what they are saying and walk away.

To argue with them is normally not productive. The truth could be a nine-thousand-pound elephant standing in front of them, and they may not see it. Some day, that elephant may just step on them.

3. Respect During a Conversation

Have you ever been talking to someone and have that person constantly sneaking a look around the room? Or have you ever tried to explain something important, such as your great accomplishments, and have the other person interrupt you with his great accomplishments? If you haven't, it's because you've never entered into a conversation with another person. Showing respect during a conversation can be boiled down to two precepts.

A. Listen—Listen—Listen

I can't count the number of times I've heard "God gave you one mouth and two ears. Therefore, you should be listening twice as much as you're talking." Still I find myself wanting to impress the person I'm talking to with how much I know and have accomplished. And over the years, I've been in enough conversations to know I'm not the only person who has that problem. There's nothing worse than feeling you have to "one up" the person you're talking to and losing the battle.

> "Instead of listening to what is being said to them, many people are already listening to what they're going to say."

Try something. During the next conversation you have with someone, focus on that person. And even if an interesting person walks by, keep looking them in the eye. And do show interest in what the other person is saying, even when they're talking about how smart their poodle is, and you wouldn't have a dog smaller than a Great Dane.

As he talks and you listen, notice how his posture and facial expression changes. Don't be surprised if he goes from crossed arms and leaning back to a much more open and inviting posture. See how his face goes from a skeptical look with a slight frown to warmth.

We're not going to spend a lot of time right now on listening because we'll be covering it quite extensively in Chapter 7 when we talk about being a good friend. However, if you follow the above suggestions, it will get you through until you get to Chapter 7.

B. Talk about the Other Person, Not You

We all like to feel important. That's why we like to impress people with everything we know and have done. I can remember a few years back when I owned a small construction-related company. I was at a party, impressing an older gentleman with my business acumen, when he was called away by the host. While waiting for someone else to impress, a friend came up and asked me if I knew who I was talking to. I said, "Yeah, Bob somebody."

My friend said, "Well, that Bob somebody just happens to be the founder and chairman of the board of a multimillion-dollar international corporation."

Embarrassed, I avoided him the rest of the evening. I wish I could say I learned my lesson, and that was the last time I tried to impress someone with what I'd accomplished or what I knew, but it wasn't so.

Too often, our conversations are like two kids yelling, "Listen to me!" "No, you listen to me!"

I've discovered that the best and easiest way to make an impact on someone is to talk about them. Think back to the last time you were impressed with the intelligence of a person with whom you had a great conversation; chances are they were intrigued with who you were.

Just recently, Sunny and I met several couples at a church gathering. As we were headed home, we started reviewing the evening and the people we met. I said, "You know, I really like Guy. He's a very intelligent and interesting person."

Sunny started asking me questions about him—things like what he did for a living, his hobbies, and where he lived. I realized I didn't know any of those things. I liked him, but I knew nothing about him. Why was he a favorite? Because he was interested in what I did for a living, my hobbies, and where I lived.

It's just as simple as this; if you want to be important, make the other person feel important.

For you hard cases, let me approach it another way. There are books out there on how to get people to do what you want them to do. The books can be summarized into a few simple statements: Be a good listener. Be interested in the other person. Talk about them, not you. Make the other person feel important. Ask questions.

This whole "respecting the other person" thing can quite possibly be summed up with a quote from a book that most of us have read a time or two: "Do unto others as you would have them do unto you."

Chapter 4

Accept Responsibility for Your Life

I was pumping fuel in my vehicle when a man in his late thirties came up to me and asked for some money so he could buy gas for his car.

I asked him why he didn't have money of his own.

He responded, "Well, it's not my fault. My wife and her lawyer took all my money when she divorced me."

"Why did she divorce you?" I asked.

"Well, she caught me running around on her. But it wasn't my fault. She wasn't a good wife."

"And you were a good husband?"

"Yes. Of course."

"Then why did you run around on her?"

"I told you it wasn't my fault."

As nice as I could, I said, "Your situation isn't my fault either. And I don't think I should be responsible for getting you out of it."

He left mumbling something about how nobody cares anymore.

When we were infants, adults were responsible for feeding us, changing our diapers, and putting us to bed. We had little or no control over our lives. As we got older, we got more control. Then as a teenager, most of us fought for total control. In reality, as a teenager, we wanted control but not responsibility. As adults, a large percentage of us still want control but not responsibility.

A while back, I saw a billboard comprised of five crying babies. Each of the babies was pointing his finger at one of the other babies. The caption read, "That's right, America. It's always someone else's fault!"

Life Isn't Fair

OK, folks, I'm going to let you in on one of the great secrets of life. Life isn't fair. We're not playing on a level field. I don't care how many laws Congress passes; the field just can't be leveled. We live on a round planet. I apologize to the "flat earth people." Every field on this planet is a part of a circle and therefore since it's an arc, that field just isn't on the level.

"The young man who thinks the world owes him a living becomes the old man who blames the world for his failure."

Just to show you how unfair life is, I'm left-handed. Statistics show left-handed people die on average nine years younger that right-handed people. That just isn't fair. And I'm considering doing something about it. I'm thinking about becoming right-handed. Incidentally, Polar bears are left-handed. This could be the real reason why they're supposedly becoming endangered.

According to Dr. Wayne Dyer, "If the world were so organized that everything had to be fair, no living creature could survive for a day. The birds would be forbidden to eat worms, and everyone's self-interest would have to be served."

When one of life's injustices, either real or perceived, comes our way, it's easy to become resentful. At one time or another, all of us have harbored resentment. We've done it because we wanted to make our failure palatable by explaining it in terms of unjust treatment by others. "If we were treated the same way . . ." "If we got the same breaks . . ." "If they weren't the bosses' pet . . ."

Resentment is a cure worse than the disease of being treated unfairly. Resentment, even when based on a real wrong, can be a habit. A bad habit. As long as we harbor resentment, it's impossible for us to look upon ourselves as a self-reliant, independent person. People who harbor resentment turn over their lives to other people.

When discussing "life's fairness" with a group of people, I often say that we could start with any person and go around the room telling stories of unfair things that have happened in our lives, and we would probably find that the next person is able to top the previous person's story.

I'm not the only person who accepts the fact that life isn't fair. A while back, Bill Gates of Microsoft fame gave a talk to a high school class. He talked about the eleven things they will not learn in school. What was the first thing on his list? "Life is not fair. Get used to it!"

The other ten are just as interesting. They're so interesting; I'm going to list them all. Each touches on an aspect of taking responsibility for our own life:

1. Life is not fair. Get used to it.
2. The world doesn't care about your self-esteem. The world will expect you to accomplish something before you feel good about yourself.
3. You will not make $60,000 a year right out of high school. You won't be a vice president until you earn it.
4. If you think your teacher is tough, wait until you get a boss.
5. Flipping burgers is not beneath your dignity. Your grandparents had a different word for burger flipping: they called it opportunity.
6. If you mess up, it's not your parents' fault, so don't whine about your mistakes; learn from them.
7. Before you were born, your parents weren't as boring as they are now. They got that way from paying your bills, cleaning your clothes, and listening to you talk about how cool you thought you were. So before you save the rain forest from the parasites of your parent's generation, try delousing the closet in your own room.

8. Your school may have done away with winners and losers, but life has not.

9. Life is not divided into semesters. You don't get summers off, and very few employers are interested in helping you find yourself.

10. Television is not real life. In real life, people actually have to leave the coffee shop and go to jobs.

11. Be nice to nerds. Chances are you'll end up working for one.

> "The Constitution guarantees you the pursuit of happiness but doesn't guarantee that you will catch up with it."

How Bad Is It Really?

It's estimated that as many as 25 percent of the world's population live in sub poverty conditions. Understand that all sub poverty conditions are not equal. The vast majority of these people have a home the size of a camping tent without a floor, they cook on an open fire, their bathroom is out behind a big tree—if there are trees in the area—and bath? Well, it does rain periodically, and education? Well, their parents did teach them how to gather their food with a spear and cook that animal over an open fire.

The very fact that you have enough of an education to be able to read this sentence means that you are more fortunate than tens of millions of people in this world. On top of that, chances are you've grown up in a country more advantaged than most, which makes you more fortunate than tens of millions of people on the planet.

Tony Robbins, the great motivator, tells the true story of W. Mitchell. Mr. Mitchell lived a life much like the rest of us until one cold night when he had an accident on his motorcycle. During the accident, the gas tank ruptured, and the sparks created by the motorcycle scraping against the highway caused the gasoline to catch fire.

Mr. Mitchell suffered third-degree burns on 65 percent of his body. Not only did he have to endure excruciating pain, it took sixteen surgeries that included grafting toes to be used as fingers. Despite the physical handicaps, Mr. Mitchell was able to fly his own plane. Not discouraged, he founded a wood-burning stove company that grew into one of Vermont's largest companies.

But as a man of great character used to say, "Here's the rest of the story." Four years after the motorcycle accident, Mr. Mitchell had a plane accident. He survived the plane accident, but his backbone was crushed, which left him paralyzed from his waist down.

If it had happened to me, I'm afraid, not only would my back be broken, so would my spirit. But not Mr. Mitchell's. He ran for mayor and was elected. His election slogan? "I'm not just another pretty face."

A while back as I was leaving the Wal-Mart parking lot, next to the street, there was a man in his mid-thirties standing with a sign that read: HOMELESS—HUNGRY—PLEASE HELP—GOD BLESS. He seemed to be in good physical shape. I wondered what caused him to end up there. I was sure it was someone else's fault.

About fifteen minutes later, as I was driving home, I saw a man jogging in the bicycle lane of the other side of the road. Actually, I looked twice because I couldn't believe what I saw the first time. This man had no legs below his knees. He was running on spring-type pieces of metal. All I could think was *Why, why, why? Why was that healthy-looking man begging for a buck or two, while the man who could have become wealthy at that spot outside the Wal-Mart parking lot was overcoming and being responsible?*

Oprah Winfrey once said, "My philosophy is that not only are you responsible for your life, but doing the best at this moment puts you in the best place for the next moment."

We all know which of these two people above were putting themselves "in the best place for the next moment."

But Bad Things Are Always Happening to Me!

Just why do some people seem to be lucky and others unlucky?

At one time, I went to a church where the minister maintained that there was no such thing as luck. He believed it to the point that we didn't have potluck meals. We had pot "providence" meals.

"Lot of good luck is undeserved, but then so is a lot of bad luck."

I'm sure you've heard the old saw "Luck is opportunity meeting preparation." If you're honest with yourself, I know you can think of several instances in your life, where an opportunity came your way, but you didn't recognize it, or maybe you weren't prepared to take advantage of it because you hadn't taken "that stupid seminar," a requirement for that opportunity.

I have a friend named Guy Lafitte. At one time, he was a consultant to casinos. He would look at the various games of chance—whether new or existing—and advise the casinos on the odds and how someone could beat the system, either legally or illegally. Although a casino could hardly keep one light bulb glowing on the money I've risked there over the years, Lafitte and I have talked a number of times about such things as what games have the best odds, and where's the best place to play the slots.

Although Lafitte doesn't encourage people to spend their time at the gambling tables or pulling the slots—after all, the odds are always in the casino's favor—he does say by playing smart, you can hang onto your grubstake a bit longer.

Maybe those people who seem to be lucky actually have studied the game of life and have figured out how to make the odds a bit more in their favor.

Many times, people talk about problems they have, when in reality, they're the problems they make.

If a corporation unexpectedly closes a plant, and everyone is laid off, an employee of that plant has a problem. On the other hand, if an employee is fired because of ineffective workmanship, that person has made the problem.

Whether you're listening to someone's problem or looking at one of yours, analyze it to see if possibly it's the one that has been made. It makes a difference.

Take something as simple as your automobile. Have you ever been late for an appointment because you couldn't find your keys? And you couldn't find your keys because you didn't put them where you normally do. Was your reaction something like, "Why do things like this always happen to me?" Did you truly not know why?

A few years back, I got a new truck. Because I had the proclivity to lock my keys in my vehicle, I normally have a "hideout" key in a very secluded place. It was a busy time in my life, so I didn't immediately get a key made. When I was at the post office, I locked my keys in my truck. Fortunately, I had road service. After berating myself to myself, I resolved to get that key. But I didn't. And wouldn't you know it, a week later, I did the same thing. Because the road service had limitations, I had to pay for this visit.

I can tell you I didn't ask myself or anyone else why it happened. I knew. I was stupid. And I can tell you within a half hour, I had that hideout key, and I haven't had that problem since.

Remember that time you hired someone to do some electrical work at your home, and he didn't show up. When you hired him, chances are you had the feeling he wasn't dependable.

I'll bet you have a friend who's undependable, yet you regularly place yourself in a position of having to depend on him.

Our brain is the world's most powerful computer. Just like a computer, it stores information. Just like a computer, it answers questions. In addition, just like a computer, it operates on the principle "Garbage in, garbage out."

This marvelous brain also has a great desire to make us happy. It wants to answer every question we ask it. No matter what the question is, if we ask the question often enough, our brain will come up with an answer. But it's the question we ask that determines the answer we get.

When we ask questions like "Why does this always happen to me?" "Why am I so unlucky?" "Why doesn't anyone like me?" our brain wants to make us happy; it will come up with an answer that isn't necessarily based on reality. The answer will be based on assumption. It's the assumption that no one likes you or that bad things always happen to you. The quality of the answers you get is less determined by the quality of your brain than the quality of the questions asked it.

We should be asking, "How can I have more friends?" "How can I make sure this unpleasant incident doesn't get repeated?" "Why" questions tend to be weak questions. "How" questions come from strength.

Isn't craziness defined as "doing the same thing over and over and expecting a different outcome?"

They're Against Me

There's a mysterious group of people who exist in the world just to create all kinds of havoc. Each of us has personally been affected by them, or we have friends who have been. That group is called the "theys." "They are against me." "They didn't give me a chance." "They don't understand me."

There are no "theys." They do not exist. It's a figment of our imagination. The next time we use "they" in this context, we need to ask ourselves the question "Who specifically are they?" If the question is answered honestly, what we will find is the "they" are either just an excuse or actually one or two specific people. If it's just an excuse, and there are no actual "theys," we have no obstacles.

However, once we have discovered specifically who "they" are, we no longer have the world against us. We have established our target. And once we have established our target, we can develop a plan on how to accomplish our objective.

Unless it specifically refers to a noun, we should eliminate "they" from our vocabulary. Also, keep in mind; the "they" may actually be "me."

Proactive vs. Reactive

Stephen Covey in his book *The Seven Habits of Highly Effective People* says proactively is "more than merely taking initiative. It means that as human beings, we are responsible for our own lives. Our behavior is a function of our decisions, not our conditions."

Reactive people are affected by their physical environment. How they feel about themselves is controlled by what happens to them. They constantly portray themselves as victims. This absolves them of any responsibility for their condition. If they wake up with a headache, it becomes an excuse for everything that goes wrong during the day. If they fail at work, the reason for this is their boss, fellow workers, or the company.

> **"Don't find fault;
> find a remedy."**

Proactive people understand headaches are a part of life. They take an aspirin and get on with it. They understand bosses, coworkers, and companies have defects, just as they do.

A proactive person makes choices based on values. A reactive person makes choices based on impulse.

It's not what happens to us but our response to what happens to us that makes the difference.

George Bernard Shaw said, "People are always blaming their circumstances for what they are. I don't believe in circumstances. The people who get on in this world are the people who get up and look for the circumstances they want, and if they can't find them, they make them."

Harland Sanders had worked hard all his life. In his sixties, he and his wife had a successful combination restaurant and gas station. Earlier he had gotten a handsome offer for the business. But he wasn't ready to retire. So he turned down the offer. Unknown to him at the time, the state was planning to build a highway, bypassing his business. At the age when he was ready to retire, Harland was broke, living on a few hundred-dollar Social Security check.

Did Harland feel sorry for himself? Did he blame the state? Possibly. But only for a short period of time. Not finding the circumstances he wanted, he made them.

Everybody loved the fried chicken he and his wife had served in their restaurant. So Harland packed a suitcase, grabbed a pressure cooker and the special spices they had used as seasoning, and took off to sell his product. Sleeping in his car, Harland called on close to a thousand restaurants before he found someone who bought his idea of their selling his fried chicken for a royalty on product sold. When he was able to accumulate enough money, Harland opened his own restaurant. It became the first of thousands of Kentucky Fried Chicken Restaurants that now circle the globe.

Remember, blaming other people and events for everything requires a lot of mental energy. It also creates stress.

> "Kicking never gets you nowhere, unless you're a mule."

Do I Have to Accept the Blame?

Understand there's a difference between responsibility and blame.

If we choose to walk down a dark alley at midnight and end up being mugged, we should accept responsibility for our choice. Although what has happened is tragic and probably involved pain and loss, by accepting responsibility, we won't look at ourselves as a victim.

Also, understand that there is a difference between responsibility and blame. We shouldn't blame ourselves for what happened. The mugging should be reported to the police. And if the mugger is caught, we should see that he's prosecuted to the fullest extent of the law. That is allowing him to take responsibility for his actions.

Guilt can be good. But too much guilt can be paralyzing. As a young person, I found there were times I had too much guilt. I can remember reading a news account of a ferryboat sinking in India resulting in a couple hundred people drowning. I found myself thinking, *Did I do something that caused that tragedy?* After I realized I, as a teenager, had no effect on this event that happened thousands of miles away, I went happily on my way guilt free. Quite possibly, my focusing on an event of great proportion thousands of miles away kept me from looking at small events that I did have control of and should have felt guilty about.

In the Crypts of Westminster Abbey, the following words are on the tomb of an Anglican bishop:

"When I was young and free and my imagination had no limits, I dreamed of changing the world. As I grew older and wiser, I discovered the world would not change, so I shortened my sights somewhat and decided to change only my country.

"But it, too, seemed immovable.

"As I grew into my twilight years, in one last desperate attempt, I settled for changing only my family, those closest to me, but alas, they would have none of it.

"And now as I lie on my deathbed, I suddenly realize if I had only changed myself first, then by example, I would have changed my family.

"From their inspiration and encouragement, I would then have been able to better my country, and who knows, I may have even changed the world."

Changing from Reactive to Proactive

Everyone has aspects about their life they don't particularly like. Those things can be changed if they're looked at in the correct manner.

If we say we're a certain way because people or circumstances have made us that way, we've given those people or circumstances the responsibility and the power for our condition. If, on the other hand, we say that we are a certain way because we have chosen to be, we've accepted the responsibility for our condition. We've also maintained the power necessary to make the changes to correct that condition.

First, we all need to understand that change isn't easy. And the older we get, the harder it is to change. We've spent a lifetime getting everything catalogued and filed away. It's like cleaning a closet. No matter how ugly the closet looks before you start cleaning it, we have to create an even bigger mess by taking everything out and putting it on the bed, the chairs, and the floor before order begins

So before we can begin cleaning the closet, we need to accept the fact that the closet is a mess.

Here's a powerful statement from Dr. Robert Schuller: "I created these problems for myself. I made decisions that caused me to be where I am today. That's why I'm facing the challenge. So I have nobody to blame but myself. That means that I'll not be angry or cynical or suspicious. I'll assume responsibility for these problems. I got myself into it. I can get myself out of it. I still believe that every obstacle is an opportunity. To learn. To grow. To be corrected or protected from making mistakes. So all this is good news. So I'm not discouraged. I'm motivated by this new challenge. I'm not depressed. I'm impressed."

Always remember, to the degree that we believe things happen to us, we are powerless. To the degree, we believe we have something to do with what happens to us, we have control over our lives.

A few years back, my brother worked for a company that was located a bit over a half-hour drive from his home. He always arrived at work five to ten minutes before "clocking in" time. In the same office was a man who literally lived across the street from the company. He perpetually arrived late for work. One day, their boss called the two of them into his office and, turning to the worker who was always late, asked, "How come Mike is always on time, and you are normally late?"

In complete seriousness, the man replied, "Well, Mike's lucky. He lives thirty minutes from work. If he leaves home late, he can make it up by driving fast. If, on the other hand, I leave home late, I can't make up the time."

It's our reaction to what happens around us, not what happens around us, that motivates us.

If you've done any white water rafting, you know how exciting it can be. On the first rapid of my first trip, I can remember the guide yelling, "Row. Row. Row fast." I didn't want to go fast. I wanted to slow down and take the rapid nice and easy.

I've since learned that if you travel down a river at or below the speed of the river's current, you have no control over where you're going. You can see the rocks and whirlpools ahead, but you have no say as to whether you hit them or go around them. By going slower than the current, you may be able to get through the rapids unscathed, but you'll look back and say, "Boy, was I lucky?"

By exceeding the speed of the current, the person operating the rudder can give direction to the raft, and the people rowing can help in making sure the raft takes the safest route through the rapids.

I remember after that first time, we gave each other "high fives" like a bunch of high school kids. We felt excited, not lucky.

That's called taking control of your life, your direction, and your destiny. Everyone encounters rocks, rapids, and whirlpools. It's a fact of life. The difference is whether we're able to leash the power of the river (life) or let it take us along randomly.

> "Some people make things happen, some watch things happen, while others wonder what has happened."

Unleashing the Power of the River

So how do I change myself from a worm to a butterfly? How can I start accepting responsibility for my life and leash this great power that life has to offer?

Let's go back to the cleaning of the closet metaphor. Cleaning the closet is usually done in two simple steps:

Step 1.   We realize and accept that the closet is a mess.
Step 2.   We need to get to work cleaning it.

1. My Closet Is Dirty

Sunny and I do a lot of traveling. For over three years, we traveled the west full time in a 34' Montana Fifth wheel called Monte. It was pulled by a one-ton Dodge Dually diesel called Hoss.

When we get ready to go somewhere, I go to my computer, get on the Internet, and click on my favorites icon called directions. To get accurate directions, I not only have to put in my final destination, I also have to put in my starting point.

By now, if we're honest with ourselves, we should have a pretty good idea as to whether we are a person who accepts responsibility for what happens in our lives or whether we duck the "R" word like the plague.

Should you need some more thought on the subject, find a place where you can get away from everyone and everything that can be a distraction to concerted thought. Don't forget to turn off your cell phone.

Just a note: If you would like to make notes while doing this exercise, do make notes. I, on the other hand, find that when I'm contemplating my navel, making notes breaks my concentration. In addition, I'm always concerned that if I or someone else notes my notes at a later date, they may not be thought noteworthy.

Get comfortable but not too comfortable; I don't want you to go to sleep. Review your day to this point. Then mentally look at yesterday, last month, and last year. Think about your successes and the times you felt on top of the world. Well, maybe not on top of the world every time, but at least, when something good happened. Think about what you did to contribute to that good thing happening, even if it's something as simple as winning a few bucks on a lottery ticket. You did contribute to it happening. You bought the ticket.

Next, think about the times things just didn't go the way you had hoped. Why didn't they?

I hope most of the time you accepted your involvement in the thing going awry. Again, we're not looking to assess guilt or blame. The object is to get an understanding of your involvement in the outcome.

2. Get to Work Cleaning Your Closet

Projects usually come in three sizes: small, medium, and large.

The small projects, like picking up our clothes, we can do in a couple of minutes and get on our way. The medium projects, like doing the weekly grocery shopping, we make a list of the items needed, find a block of time to go shopping, decide whether to go to Wal-Mart or Safeway, make sure we have enough money in our checking account; and then get on with it.

The big projects, we put off as long as possible. Over the years, if there was such a thing as a frustration meter, I believe it would register the highest when I had a large project in front of me, such as writing this book.

Some wise person—obviously from Africa or India—asked the question and gave the answer to this situation. The question: "How do you eat an elephant?" Answer: "One bite at a time."

If you find that taking responsibility is a small problem, then, there is no problem. If it's a medium problem, awareness should be sufficient to motivate you to make corrections. If you have an elephant in front of you, start by taking small bites.

Both mentally and verbally, get rid of such phrases as "why does this always happen to me?" "With my luck" . . . you know the rest of the phrases. Then start analyzing just why things went wrong. Again, I emphasize, you don't have to take the blame, but your share of the responsibility.

People who have studied these things say it takes twenty-one days to change a habit. Maybe it's because I'm not as smart as people who have studied these things, but it often takes me twenty-one weeks to change some of my habits. The main thing is not to get discouraged. Every day, take a bite. You'll be surprised how fast that elephant disappears.

Earlier, we quoted Robert Schuller. At this point, I think we should do it again. If each day you repeat the following with conviction, I can assure you that elephant will disappear in no time:

> The world won't give me a living—
>> If it's going to be, it's up to me.
> Society won't give me moral and ethical character—
>> If it's going to be, it's up to me.
> The university will not give me an education—
>> If it's going to be, it's up to me.
> Business doesn't owe me a job—
>> If it's going to be, it's up to me.
> Psychology can't give me joy and happiness—
>> If it's going to be, it's up to me.
> Religious institutions will not save my soul—
>> If it's going to be, it's up to me.
> The minister who unites me in marriage to my spouse won't give me
>> a lifetime of happiness and harmony—
>> If it's going to be, it's up to me.

The medical establishment can't give me good health—
    If it's going to be, it's up to me.
The national economy will not deliver financial security to my purse—
    If it's going to be, it's up to me.
A new sunrise doesn't promise to give me a great day—
    If it's going to be, it's up to me.

"Knowledge is power." We probably remember our parents or some teacher telling us this as a means of encouraging us to study. But is it true? Is knowledge really power? During our lifetime, I'm sure we've all experienced knowing someone extremely knowledgeable, who spent their life accumulating knowledge and doing nothing with it.

When I was young, my father took me by a shack with no electricity or water. Once inside, I discovered the interior walls were cardboard. For insulation, the occupant had stuffed newspaper between the cardboard and exterior walls. The occupant was a fifty-year-old ex-college professor with two doctor's degrees. During our two-hour conversation, he spoke very eloquently. I'm not exactly sure of his problem. Obviously, he had chosen not to be a participant in society. He had knowledge but no power because he wasn't using his knowledge.

Knowledge isn't power. Knowledge is only "potential" power. You now have the knowledge. Turn it into power. Accept responsibility for your life.

3. Getting Your Master's Degree

Now that we've agreed to accept responsibility for our lives, let's go one step further and, not only accept responsibility for the bad things, but sharing the responsibility for the good things that happen.

One of the greatest team builders of this century was a football coach from Alabama by the name of Paul "Bear" Bryant. According to Coach Bryant, this is how he did it:

"I'm just a plow-hand from Arkansas, but I have learned how to hold a team together. How to lift some men up and how to calm down others until finally they've got one heartbeat together, a team. There's just three things I'd ever say:

"If anything goes bad, I did it. If anything goes semi-good, then we did it. If anything goes real good, then you did it. That's all it takes to get people to win football games for you."

You may never step near a football field, but you are a member of a team. That team may be at work, church, a social club, or your family. Accepting responsibility when things go bad and sharing responsibility when they go well is a real winner. Do you think you can do it?

Accepting Responsibility Empowers

A vital element in the lives of most successful people throughout history is their accepting responsibility, not only for what they've done, but what they will become.

Few people become a leader without accepting responsibility, and none stay there without continuing to accept responsibility. Personal responsibility is paramount for leadership. When a person has the integrity of accepting responsibility, that person's self-esteem increases their ability to accomplish more. And when a person accomplishes more, they become more successful.

So by taking responsibility for your life, your self-esteem will increase, increasing your self-respect and achievement.

Accepting Responsibility Makes You Free

We've talked earlier about how not taking responsibility for your life puts your life's outcome in the hands of other people. And that is true whether we place responsibility for our lives in the hands of someone else or the government.

Accepting responsibility for your life doesn't mean you'll have an easy life. It means you'll be free.

When I was a young man, I was told a story that does a great job of illustrating just what freedom is and is not. The story goes like this:

A yellow canary sits on its perch in a cage by a window. Its water and seed cups are full. The room in which the canary's cage is located is kept warm during the winter and cool during the summer. To protect the canary from light and other inconvenience at night, a cover is placed over the cage. With its cage hanging from a ceiling hook, the canary is protected from the house cat. The canary's every need is anticipated.

"Look, Professor, it's not *my* fault I failed your class. It's *your* fault for not motivating me."

Outside the window on a bare branch sits a sparrow. There's a foot of snow on the ground. The sparrow will have to fly long distances to find the seed and insects necessary to satisfy its hunger. While looking for food, it has to watch for feral cats, raccoons, and skunks that are also looking for food.

The question is "Which bird is free?" It very well could be that each time we give someone else responsibility for an aspect of our life, we're losing a piece of our freedom.

Chapter 5

Be Positive and Cheerful

Whether in a bunkhouse or on a cattle drive, there was little that got an Old West cowboy on the "outs" than to be constantly complaining about his horses, the food, or the working conditions. If he were on a trail drive, the cowboy would probably have one other thing to complain about—dust—because he would be relegated to riding drag, the worst job on a trail drive. If he were at the ranch, he would probably be sleeping in the barn with the horses.

For some people being positive and cheerful brings to mind a Pollyanna, someone who looks at life through rose-colored glasses or maybe someone who goes around, handing out flowers and saying, "Peace. Love."

Optimism is sometimes looked upon as unrealistic. According to psychologists at Pittsburgh's Carnegie Mellon University, optimists see the world just as clearly as pessimists do. The difference is that to an optimist, a problem or setback is simply something to overcome, not a defeat.

A person who is positive and cheerful has to be tough with a high level of durability. If you're like me, you find it difficult to keep negative thoughts out of your head for any period of time. This is because our lives are inundated every day with negativity. It begins with our turning on the radio in the morning or reading the newspaper. The policy of any newscast or newspaper is "If it bleeds, it leads." So the first thing in the morning, we're told the worst that has happened since the last time we heard or read the worst that had happened since the previous time we heard or read the worst that had happened.

The best way to avoid having your comments being aired on TV or the radio about being involved in a catastrophe of nature is to acknowledge what happened and express that you, your family, and friends are working hard at cleaning up the mess and repairing the damage. Then to put a nail in the coffin, express your thanks to God that everyone came through the catastrophe safely. And everyone's safety is much more important than what happened to things.

Everybody knows "good news" doesn't sell. And with the number of twenty-four-hour news channels on TV, sometimes there just isn't enough bad news to go around.

I remember a TV newscaster who led off the news segment with "Experts say an asteroid is scheduled to hit the earth! Total destruction forecasted. We'll have this story right after this break." Why do they always have to have a commercial before telling us catastrophic news?

When they came back to the news, the newscaster interviewed an expert, who said that mathematically within the next thousand years, an asteroid could possibly hit the earth and cause catastrophic destruction.

> "Pessimists are all alike; they are always good for bad news."

I had just spent three minutes in sheer terror, watching deodorant and insurance commercials only to discover that some unknown scientist from some obscure university had worked out a mathematical formula showing sometime over the next thousand years—that's ten centuries, one hundred decades, I don't know how many generations—an asteroid could possibly hit the earth, and it would quite possibly destroy a large portion of the earth. I had a hard time passing high school algebra, but I believe chances of my being hit and killed crossing the street are greater than my being killed by that asteroid. Now I'm worried about crossing the street.

"Negative thoughts are like birds. We can't stop them from landing on our heads, but we can certainly stop them from building nests in our hair."

Someone has estimated that during the period of a day, 80 percent of the verbal and nonverbal messages we receive are negative. I haven't seen that person's research data, so I'm not sure how he came up with 80 percent, but I can guarantee we get more negative than positive vibes.

It's Our Parents Fault

I know what you're saying. "Wasn't the whole previous chapter dedicated to telling us not to blame others for our condition?" You're correct. I was just testing you.

However, unless your parents were a lot more patient than mine were and than I was as a parent, your training took place by being told what not to do over and over and over again. And not always just verbally.

When you learned what you were supposed to do and you did it, they might have said, "That's good, Johnny." But, very quickly, good behavior was just accepted as normal. It was almost as if we had to continually search out the bad so that we would know it was something we shouldn't do.

"A pessimist enjoys having something to worry about because if he didn't have anything to worry about, he'd be even more worried."

Tony Robins maintains—and I believe he's correct—that pain is a greater motivator than pleasure. When he wants to motivate someone, he has them think about not only what it would be like not to make that sale, but what their family and they personally would be if they didn't do the thing they know they should.

So that's what we're going to do. We're not only going to look at the benefits of optimism but the downside of pessimism.

Benefits of Optimism vs. Pessimism

Some people refuse to fly. Others don't like to fly but do it anyway. I don't mind flying, even though each time I see a plane, whether on the ground or in the air, I tell myself there is no way that big thing, weighing tons and tons, can fly through the air with the greatest of ease. I'm still convinced it's an illusion.

Like everyone who has flown very much, I've had good and bad experiences. Fortunately, the bad experiences haven't included sitting on the tarmac for hours or one of those thousand-foot instant drops in altitude.

The interesting thing is no matter whether I choose to have a good experience or a bad experience while flying, my experience has nothing to do with the time I arrive at my destination. Good or bad, I'm there at the same time.

So why not ignore the crying baby two rows up, the fact that only a middle seat was available when we checked in, or the virtual strip search I had to go through at security?

Incidentally, I hope you understand that in the above illustration, taking a trip on a plane is a metaphor. What I'm really talking about is life and how, whether we're pessimistic or optimistic, we get to the end of life at the same time. However, in actuality, that's not absolutely true. Optimistic people do live longer. For pessimistic people, life just seems to be longer.

Some of us feel if we just had a bigger house or newer automobile, we would be happy. Then there are those people with the bigger house and new automobile, who feel what they need is a vacation home and a sporty second car. We all see the commercials where people are happy because they're drinking a certain brand of beer or vacationing on a Caribbean island.

The sad thing is these items rarely make us as happy as we have hoped. Psychologists have attached a name to this phenomenon. It's called affective forecasting. The truth be told, no matter how much we make or how many toys we have, if we're not happy inside, these won't make us happy.

So what are the benefits of optimism over pessimism? Let's turn to the experts. Researchers followed over 1,700 healthy adults for a period of ten years just to see how the lives of those who regularly experience depression, hostility, and anxiety differed from those who regularly experienced joy, happiness, and excitement.

Before we get too far into this, understand that positive and cheerful people do, at times, experience depression and other negative emotions. The difference is that when a pessimist is overcome with negativity, they quit. When an optimist has negative emotions, their basic optimistic outlook gives them enough extra energy to crest the hill and coast to success.

So what have the experts discovered are the benefits of being positive and cheerful?

1. Mental Benefits

Have you ever known a "worry wart?" Someone who always expects the worst? They believe that by expecting the worst, they won't be surprised when it or something less than the worst comes along. For them, a minor inconvenience is a disaster. A few minutes of frustration ruins their whole day. Fortunately, there aren't many "worry warts" in the world. So they're easy to avoid. And people do avoid them. This helps the "worry wart" fulfill the worry that they don't have friends.

> "Fortunately, there aren't many 'worry warts' in the world."

We all worry at times. Sometimes when things are just going too good, we worry that the other shoe is going to drop any time. We get a great job, develop a new friendship, or just go a few days without a disaster in our lives, and we start worrying that it's going to end. This creates two effects in our lives. First, what we're saying to ourselves is that we don't deserve the job, friend, or a life void of disaster. And anytime we don't feel we deserve something, we won't keep it. We do things to sabotage the job, friendship, or peaceful life. Second, by worrying about losing the things that make us happy, we don't enjoy them while we have them.

By enjoying fully the good things in our lives, we not only make our today more pleasant, we ensure those things that give us pleasure today are cultivated, so they'll be with us tomorrow.

Dusty was making his first solo parachute jump from a plane. As the plane was approaching the jump zone, the instructor ran through the procedure one more time.

"There are four things you need to remember. First, when I tell you to jump, you jump. Second, wait for five seconds and pull the rip cord. Third, if the main chute doesn't open, pull the emergency chute rip cord. And fourth, when you land, the truck will be there to pick you up."

The instructor said "jump," and Dusty jumped. After five seconds, he pulled the rip cord. The chute didn't open. He then pulled the emergency rip cord. It didn't open either. As Dusty was in free fall, he was heard to say, "With my luck, I bet the truck won't be there either."

Is being positive that the truck won't be there a positive or a negative attitude? It's a bit like we said earlier; if you try to fail and you fail, have you succeeded?

At one time, it was thought that people's brains were either wired for them to be happy or not. Now it's felt that this isn't necessarily so.

> "If you try to fail and you fail; have you succeeded?"

However, there are those who very well could be mentally predisposed in one direction or another, like the twin boys—since birth, one was an absolute pessimist and the other was an incurable optimist. To make them "normal," a psychologist suggested putting the pessimist in a room full of the latest toys and the optimist in a room of horse manure. That would make the one more optimistic and the other more realistic.

After a couple of hours, the psychologist went into the room full of toys. The pessimistic boy was crying. The psychologist asked why.

The boy said, "With all these new toys, I can't decide which one to play with first, and when I do decide, I'll probably break it."

The psychologist then went into the room full of horse manure. The optimistic boy was standing in the middle of the room, laughing and digging through the manure.

"What are you doing?" asked the psychologist.

The boy responded, "With all this manure, there has to be a pony here somewhere."

The ancient Greeks believed an enthusiast was a God-intoxicated person—a person who God drives to become exceptional. Enthusiasm has also been described as knowledge on fire.

Don't confuse enthusiasm with excitement. Excitement tends to come from some outside stimulus. People get excited at football games. We get excited about going on a vacation. It's something that happens to us.

Enthusiasm springs from the inside. Nothing is as contagious as enthusiasm. When a person is enthusiastic, he/she makes other people excited.

We're all familiar with the "placebo effect." That's, when we're given a sugar pill and told it's a powerful medication that will cure our illness, and even though it's a sugar pill, we believe it, and our illness is cured.

There is also something called a nocebo effect. That's, when we have a negative belief or attitude, then against all odds, we produce negative results.

The boy in the above illustration may not find a horse, but he'll sure have fun, looking.

Creative people, who are positive, are always willing to look at things differently. A man with no experience in the drilling industry was appointed the president of a drill bit company. Shortly after taking over the company, he met with his manufacturing staff and sales force and declared, "We will no longer sell drill bits. From this time forward, we will sell holes."

This subtle change in the way the company looked at what they did resulted in a dramatic increase in sales and profit by their developing and selling a large variety of ways to "create holes."

2. Physical Benefits

According to the *Journal of Personality and Social Psychology*, a person's optimism or pessimism could affect their immune system. The report showed that the levels of T-cells, a measurement of immunity, rose by 13 percent when optimists faced a challenge but dropped 3 percent when pessimists faced the same challenge.

Scientists say every day our body produces cancerous cells. Our body also has killer cells to destroy the cancerous cells. Fear, worry, anxiety, and stress weaken the killer cells, making us more susceptible to the bad guys.

Dr. Kenneth Cooper, in his book *Regaining the Power of Youth*, says, "If you believe that you will be energetic and youthful on a given day, the chances are that you will indeed possess more vigor. On the other hand, if you begin the day thinking about your aches and pains and fatigue, your outlook will be precisely the opposite."

The researchers also discovered that no one's pessimism is written in stone. A person can become more optimistic by taking a pessimistic thought and consciously transforming it into an optimistic one.

During the study of those 1,700 people that we talked about earlier, the researchers found the happiest people were 22 percent less likely to develop heart disease than those who were in the middle of the scale. In addition, even when optimistic people were going through tough times, their heart attack "immunity" persisted.

Everyone gets discouraged. A study of successful people shows that at some point every one of them became discouraged—some quite often. At times, it seemed as if everything was against them, or even when they experienced success, they encountered some personal tragedy. Yet they kept going and succeeded.

Just remember, when you're running up hill, it's all right to give up as many times as you would like, as long as your legs keep propelling you up hill.

3. Social Benefits

Sometime during each of our lives, we've encountered someone who is negative about everything. I knew someone like that when I was in college. His name was Larry Gray. We called him Granny Gray because we felt he was crotchety like a grandmother—my apologies to grandmothers. I'm married to a grandmother, and she is anything but crotchety. Then, what do you know when you're in your early twenties?

Anyway, when we were going after pizza, Granny Gray would virtually beg to go and then the whole time complain about his being with us and not somewhere else. According to him, the food at the cafeteria was terrible, but he always ate there. About the only thing he didn't complain about was the small group of friends who tolerated him. Today, I wouldn't put up with it. Why did we put up with it then? We thought he was funny. Then, what do you know when you're in your early twenties?

When we have a problem in our lives, we often have the desire to tell all our friends and everyone we encounter about the problem. It can be therapeutic and helpful to solving the problem to talk to a close friend or relative about it but not the whole world.

There's a cowboy saying that goes like this: "It's best to keep your troubles pretty much to yourself. 'Cause half the people you tell 'em to won't give a darn and the other half will be glad to hear you got 'em."

Understand we may not complain all the time, but when we do, it stands out like a sore thumb.

> **"Never grumble. It makes you about as welcome as a sidewinder in a cow camp."**

A Catholic priest entered a celibate Italian monastery. The monks had to live in virtual silence. However, they were allowed to say two words at the end of each two-year period. Although the young monk worked hard and obeyed all the rules of the monastery, he had a difficult time.

After the first two years, he said, "Bad bed." After the second two years, he said, "Bad food." At the end of six years, he said, "I quit."

The head of the monastery said, "It doesn't surprise me. All you've done since you've been here is complain, complain, complain."

Isn't it interesting how sometimes our words speak a lot louder than our actions?

If we go about talking doom and gloom that we do not believe in ourselves and that we have little respect for ourselves, we cannot blame other people for taking us at our own estimate.

Another social phoneme is that whether we're pessimistic or optimistic, we draw people of a similar attitude to us.

An old prospector was camped alongside of a stream next to a road that led into a small frontier town.

A young man on a horse came down the road and pulled up next to the stream to let his horse have a drink. He asked the prospector, "What kind of people live here?"

The prospector asked, "What kind of people lived in the place where you just left?"

"They were a bad lot," replied the young man. "I was glad to leave them."

"You'll find the same here," said the prospector.

Later, another man came by, pulled up his horse, and asked the prospector the same question. The prospector also asked him about the people who lived in the town he had just left.

With a smile on his face he said, "They were great people. Honest. Friendly."

"You'll find the same here," replied the prospector.

A man, fishing the stream nearby, heard both conversations. He took his line out of the water and walked over to the prospector. "Those two men asked you the same question, but you gave them a different answer. How can you give a completely different answer to the same question?"

The prospector explained, "Each person carries within him the environment in which he lives. No matter where we go, people are the same. People are to us what we ourselves find in them."

In no way do I support using people, but the story of Tom Sawyer shows another element of being positive and cheerful. As you will remember, Tom Sawyer was given the job of painting his fence. He had two choices: Grumble and complain while he did the job or do it cheerfully and enthusiastically. He chose the latter. And what happened? His friends saw how much fun he was having and wanted to join in. Tom Sawyer ended up sitting back and watching his friends paint the fence.

The interesting thing is that being friendly; smiling at a stranger; asking someone with conviction, "How are things going?" and then listening, not only helps the recipient, it helps the giver. Even walking around with a smile on your face makes people feel better. If nothing else, they'll wonder why you're smiling.

It's hard to imagine what would happen if we would live our lives with joy on our face and passion in our heart.

Becoming Optimistic

I hope, at this point, anyone who isn't inclined to be optimistic has gotten the point and is seriously considering this "optimism" thing.

So just how does one change from pessimism to being positive and cheerful. We looked at what the experts had to say about the benefits of optimism. Let's consult them again on how to become that which we've been promoting.

Taking the lead from the old Jack Nicholson movie *Five Easy Pieces*, here are the five easy steps.

1. Be Grateful

An airline flight was traveling over Colorado. The businessman, sitting next to the window, spoke to his associate in the middle seat, "See that lake we're flying over? When I was a kid, I fished that lake. I would look up at the planes flying overhead and dream about some day being a passenger in one of those planes. Now I fly over that lake and dream about sitting on its bank and fishing. I guess I didn't know what I had when I had it."

"I guess I didn't know what I had when I had it."

Back in the olden days of our prehistoric ancestors, when there were "lions and tigers and bears, Oh My!" in order to survive, our brains had to focus on all those dangerous things lurking about. And those who were most likely to survive focused so intently that they ignored the things that weren't hurtful or in other words, pleasant.

Obviously, each of our ancestors did the survival thing well, or we wouldn't be here now. For some of us, more than others, we still have that trait running through our genes.

We get so wrapped up in trying to survive: Maintaining our job; keeping the bill collector from our door; and the other lions and tigers and bears, that we miss appreciating the great things we do have, like a job, children and spouse, and even a home with a door from which we can try to keep bill collectors away.

Dr. Norman Vincent Peale had a man come to him complaining about all the problems in his life. Dr. Peale asked the man if he would like to get rid of his problems. The man responded, "I sure would."

Dr. Peale said, "I'll take you to a place where no one has a problem and you can decide if you want to join them."

Dr. Peale drove to a cemetery and pointed out no one buried there had a problem.

He concluded by saying, "Since dead people have no problems, the more problems you have, the more alive you are."

I don't think Dr. Peale was suggesting that each of us try to create as many problems as possible for ourselves. But it's the way we look at problems.

If we're alive, problems are inevitable. There's no way of getting around it. If we spend our lives worrying about the lions and tigers and bears, there is no way life can even be endurable.

Mark Twain said, "I've been through some terrible things in my life. Some of which actually happened." We're all bridge builders. And like Mark Twain, a large percentage of those bridges we never cross.

You're better off than you think. If you have food in the refrigerator, clothes on your back, a roof over your head, and a place to sleep, you're richer than 75 percent of the people in this world. If you have money in the bank, or in your wallet, you're among the 8 percent richest people in the world. The very fact you're reading this means you're better off than the two billion people in the world who can't read.

> "I've been through some terrible things in my life. Some of which actually happened."
> —Mark Twain

2. Practice Being Optimistic

There is no one as optimistic as the young boy who, anxious for the beginning of little league baseball season, took his bat and ball into his backyard and, with an underhand motion, threw the ball in the air. As it came back down, he swung the bat. Whiff. He missed the ball. "Strike one," he said to himself. He threw it up a second time. Again, he missed the ball. "Strike two." As he reached down to pick up the ball, there was a slight smile on his face. A third time he threw the ball in the air. Again, all that could be heard was the whiff of the bat cutting the air. "Strike three."

The young boy now had a big smile on his face. "Boy, am I going to be a great pitcher." he said to himself.

> "The vast majority of the problems we encounter are not catastrophes."

The vast majority of the problems we encounter are not catastrophes. Remember the last time you were with a group of old friends? You spent the evening, remembering the times you had together. Everyone had several stories to relate. The stories were always of fun things that happened years before. You even talked about those times that weren't funny when they happened; some even of a tragic nature were either laughed about or remembered with ambivalence.

How often do we go through an event that ranges from an inconvenience to an outright tragedy, only to find a couple of years later we're relating the incident to someone as an amusing story or one of life's lessons? This is more normal than not.

Why not use this as an aid to help you get through an uncomfortable or tragic time? Look at the traumatic event as a possible story or life experience you'll be relating to someone in two years. This attitude allows you to not only look at what you're experiencing more calmly, it also lets you analyze your feelings more rationally. You'll be relieved of some of the panic of the experience, and what's more important, you'll understand the event isn't the end of your life.

Every positive, upbeat person I know exercises. Aerobic exercise creates better physical health. It decreases health worries and provides an escape from the day's problems. Exercise also creates endorphins, those mood-elevating chemicals that are released by the brain during exercise. These endorphins lift our moods, release our stress, and calm our minds.

The problem is the time we most need the magic of endorphins is the very time when we're least motivated to exercise. When we're depressed or overwhelmed with the obligations of life, we want to either wallow in our misery or feel we need to spend all our time working to stay ahead.

We need to force ourselves to take a thirty-minute walk. This can produce enough endorphins to create an upbeat mood and increase our productivity beyond the time spent on walking. At this point, I would like to thank my dog, Jake, because even when I want to stay in my warm home away from the cold, he stays after me until we go on our morning walk. Maybe you need a Jake, even if he's a human being.

Each day, a patient who occupied a hospital bed next to a window would describe the outside activities to his roommate, who was unable to look out the window. The roommate looked forward each day to learning what was going on in the "real" world. It took his mind off the pain he was experiencing. When the patient next to the window died, his friend asked to move to the bed next to the window so he could experience the joy of seeing the outside activities first hand. Using all the energy he could muster, he raised himself, looked out the window, and saw nothing but a block wall. His roommate had been describing the beautiful days and the grassy lawn with children playing on it from memory.

"Everybody needs a Jake"

Sometimes, what we perceive reality to be can be more powerful than reality. Now, I'm not suggesting that we move into a world of fantasy. Yet there have been a couple of times I've passed a street person talking to themself using incomprehensible phrases and have a twinge of envy for the world in which they are living.

When we practice optimism, even when facing a block wall, we will find our optimism will affect other people in a positive way. The benefit to us? First, even on down days, when we stop thinking about ourselves and turn our attention to helping others, we'll find when we raise the self-esteem of someone else; we can't help but raise our own self-esteem. Our seeing other people become positive and cheerful because of our actions makes us feel better about ourselves, and guess what, we become genuinely positive and cheerful.

3. Visualize Your Best

Nathaniel Hawthorne, the author of *The Scarlet Letter* and *the House of the Seven Gables,* also wrote a short story called *The Great Stone Face.*

It tells of a village at the foot of a mountain in which "nature in her mood of majestic playfulness" formed the features of a man. Legend said, "One day a child should be born thereabouts, who was destined to become the greatest and noblest personage of his time, and whose countenance, in manhood, should bear the exact resemblance to the great stone face."

A young man named Ernest became enthralled with the legend. He spent his life looking at the great stone face and imagining how the "greatest and noblest personage would act." During his lifetime, a great landowner was declared the legend, then a great soldier, and finally a politician. Each was later determined to be a mistake.

During all this time, Ernest continued his passion of looking upon the great stone face and imagining how the person would act. The story ends with Ernest, the humble villager, being declared the true likeness of the great stone face by the whole village.

Our imaginations are very powerful. I know people who imagine planes crashing to the point they refuse to get on one. You can show them facts such as driving to their destination are much more dangerous than flying. With their time constraints, three hours on a plane verses three days driving will give them much more time to be productive.

You can even show them a spreadsheet showing the cost effectiveness of flying, but you might as well be talking to a fence post. No matter what you say, they will not get on a plane.

I have a friend who absolutely loved the ocean until she saw the movie *Jaws*. Now she will spend time on the beach and even go in the ocean up to her knees, as long as she's surrounded by other people, who she imagines the shark has to consume before it gets to her. The fact that no one has been killed by a shark in the ocean off the beach of Newport Beach, California, means nothing to her.

Dr. Dennis Waitley, one of the world's best-known performance authors and speakers, tells the story of POW Colonel George Hall, who was a four-handicap golfer prior to being captured.

While imprisoned in an eight-by-eight cell, each day, he would play a round of golf in his head. He imagined every drive, every fairway shot, chip shot, and putt. At the end of the round, his score would match his handicap.

Shortly after his being released, he played the New Orleans Open. His score? Seventy-six, four over par. Over the years, Colonel Hall had created a pattern in his mind.

One of the many fascinating things about our mind is that if our subconscious vividly imagines something, our conscious mind and our body will react as if what was imagined is actually true.

When many people think about visualization and meditation, an Indian guru with crossed legs is pictured. To them, it's more inaction than action. A bumper sticker expresses the feelings of these people quite well. "Visualize whirled peas."

I must admit, there is a bit of that kind of a person in me. Each time I have been in a situation where someone is instructing me and others about how to meditate, I always find those things the person wants me to visualize are not the things I enjoy visualizing. In addition, they're always going too fast or too slow. OK, I know I'm an insensitive contrarian.

If the traditional style of meditation works for you, go for it. My attempt is not to discourage anyone. My attempt is to get more people involved by using different terminology and methodology.

The person who wouldn't fly and the person who was afraid of the ocean didn't get there because of meditation. They got there as a result of their imagination. Because of some experience or information, their imagination imagined danger so real that no matter how many facts are laid out in front of them, they refuse to believe them.

Gary Zukav, in his book *The Seat of the Soul*, says, "The club that kills can drive a stake into the ground to hold a shelter. The spear that takes a life can be used as a lever to ease life's burdens. The knife that cuts flesh can be used to cut cloth. The hands that build bombs can be used to build schools. The minds that coordinate the activities of violence can coordinate the activities of cooperation."

Although he didn't mention it, the imagination that keeps us from doing something totally logical can also motivate us to do great things.

I came across this idea while listening to Tony Robins. As indicated earlier, Tony maintains, and rightfully so, that if we vividly imagine something, it will be as if we actually experience it. Our subconscious cannot differentiate between what is vividly imagined and what is actually experienced.

So how do you do it? First, find a place where you feel comfortable and mentally get away from what is happening right now.

Make sure there aren't distractions—no phones, no TV, and no yelling kids. Turn off that cell phone. The place can be your back deck or your den, or if you're fortunate like I am to live in a forested area, go into the woods and sit under a pine tree. I often wake up in the middle of the night and find myself to be in a contemplative mood.

When you are in this magical location, begin to turn off the outside world. In the movie *For the Love of the Game,* while throwing a perfect game, the pitcher, played by Kevin Costner, would say to himself, "Clear the mechanism," and in his head, the noise from the crowd would disappear, and there would be total silence.

It's not always that simple for me and may not be for you. Even for Kevin Costner, later in the game, the mechanism stopped working. Nevertheless, he kept pitching.

At whatever point you're at, if you're in the moment enough to feel comfortable, start thinking about pleasant things that are in your life or pleasant things that you've experienced.

Don't think about unpleasant things or people. At this point, don't even think about thinking about anything unpleasant. Because when we try not to think about something, we are actually thinking about it. It's like me telling you not to think about an elephant. When you read that previous sentence, I'll bet you thought about an elephant.

Our brains think at about 1,200 words per minute. What we want to do is to slow it down a bit.

By now, you should be feeling pretty mellow. Here's where you start working. Begin thinking about the things you want to accomplish.

> "Here's where you start working."

Language is very important, even the language we use when we talk to ourselves. Too often, we simply lay out our goals or wishes about what we would like to accomplish.

We say to ourselves, "I want to stop procrastination." "Some day I'll get all my bills paid off." On the other hand, "I would sure like to fix things up around my place." What we are actually saying is that we want to do these things, but we just don't think we have what it takes to accomplish them.

Instead, we need to say, "I will stop procrastinating." "I intend to get all my bills paid off." In addition, "I am going to fix things up around my place."

This changes our mental attitude from one of wishing and hoping to one of being in the process of making it happen.

We have what we want in life, not what we think we want but what we really want.

It's been said that we have about fifty thousand thoughts per day. As stated earlier, the majority of our encounters and thoughts are negative. So what do we do about the negative thoughts? First, it isn't whether or not we're having the negative thoughts; it's what we do with them when we have them. Do we ponder and spend time thinking about them? Or do we dismiss them?

Realize when we have a thought—good or bad—that's all it is: a thought. It can't hurt or help us unless we get into it. We've all been in a situation where we remember an unpleasant encounter that took place years ago. Before long, we're getting angry. We're mentally kicking ourselves for the things we did or didn't do. And emotionally we feel as if it just happened.

On the other hand, when a negative thought comes into our head, we can dismiss it immediately by visualizing it getting smaller and moving to the back of our head. At first, it may be a bit difficult, but as we practice it, this becomes easier.

Then again, when we get a positive thought, like the fact you're loved by your spouse, nourish the thought.

4. Forgive and Forget

"Good judgment comes from experience, and a lot of that comes from bad judgment."

A Piece of String, a short story by Guy de Maupassant, tells of a man named Naitre Hauchecorne, who picked up a piece of string while walking through a marketplace. A wallet had been lost at the same time and place. Someone saw Hauchecorne pick up the string and thought he had picked up the missing wallet. Although he protested and showed them the string, the authorities took Hauchecorne to the police station.

The next day, the owner found the wallet. Everyone forgot the incident, but Naitre Hauchecorne never forgot. He complained about the injustice to everyone he encountered. It became his life. He neglected his farm and lost everything, including his friends. Self-pity destroyed him. Naitre Hauchecorne died of a broken heart, complaining to the end about the piece of string.

When we refuse to forgive and forget, we actually hurt ourselves more than we hurt the other person.

Research shows the physical and the psychological reactions of not being able to forgive and forget causes blood to clot more quickly and inhibits digestion, and it can even be a major contribution to a stroke or heart attack.

One could almost say not forgiving and forgetting is sort of like shooting yourself and expecting the other person to bleed to death.

Also, remember the Biblical admission not to judge others so you won't be judged yourself. I believe the Bible was talking about more than just God judging us. I believe there is also an element of our judging and not forgiving others, making it easier for others who know of our attitude to justify their judging and not forgiving us.

Forgetting? OK, so you can't forget. Just agree with yourself that you're not going to think about it all the time. Don't become another Naitre Hauchecorne.

At the same time you're being forgiving, don't be dumb. Just because an abusing spouse always asks for forgiveness after abusing you, doesn't mean you should stick around for another round of abuse. Forgive the person, and get out of there.

So a friend or a child has borrowed money from you in the past with promises to pay you back and didn't. And they come to you again with the same promise. Even if you have the money in a shoebox rotting away, it may just be best for them if you use a bit of "tough love."

> "If you lend someone $20 and never see that person again, it was probably worth it."

5. Choose Your Friends Wisely

A while back, I heard a news item about an innovative method of building homes with straw. The straw is used as insulation with wood framing and stuccoed to give the straw sturdiness.

The builder talked about the straw being inexpensive and light and that it conserved resources.

Wrapping up the story, the reporter asked, "Just what does this say about the story of the wolf and the straw house built by one of the pigs?"

The contractor replied, "The story doesn't say that you shouldn't build a house with straw but that you shouldn't let pigs build it."

Think about it. It could be that the reason your last idea failed wasn't that it was a bad idea, but the failure was because of the people you chose to help you accomplish it.

If you look for people who are positive and cheerful, fair in their dealings, people of their word, and willing to go the distance, then your project will be an assured success.

> "Some people can take the most positive situation and turn it into a negative one."

And your life is the same. If you want your life to be successful, you need to avoid people who are always seeing the glass half-empty and constantly belittling you, others, and themselves.

Some people can take the most positive situation and turn it into a negative one. Like the guy who invited a new friend to go duck hunting. The host was very proud of his bird dog. They went out on the lake in a small boat and waited. After a while, a flock of ducks came over. Bang, bang. One of the ducks broke formation and landed fifty yards from the boat. "Now, let me show you what my dog can do," said the host. And he sent his dog after the duck. The dog jumped out of the boat and walked on top of the water out to the duck, fetched the duck, and walked on the water back to the boat, releasing the duck in the hunter's hand. With a big smile on his face, the host asked the guest, "What do you think about my dog?" The guest responded, "What's wrong? Can't you teach the dog how to swim?"

As we talked about earlier, a vast majority of stimulus we receive in life is negative. Much of it we can't control, but our friends, we sure can control. If, on a regular basis, we feel down or depressed when we leave the presence of someone, we need to get rid of them.

If, on the other hand, we feel good when we leave the presence of someone, cultivate his or her friendship.

And finally, always remember whether you're positive and cheerful or a grouch, it's up to you.

You must take the advice of a famous twelve-step program and live your life one day at a time. Wake up each morning and say, "Thank you, God, for giving me another day." Life is just too short not to enjoy every single day.

There are going to be days when things go wrong. That's inevitable. I attack the problems and keep thinking, *If it wasn't for these bad days, I wouldn't really be able to enjoy the great days.* The storms allow us to appreciate the days of sunshine. And even in the midst of a storm, remember the sun's just waiting to pop out.

Chapter 6

Be a Person of Your Word

Of all the precepts of the Old West cowboy's code, the one that is originally stated, "Let your handshake be your bond," was the most important. Even Hollywood realized this as they made movies like *High Noon* with Gary Cooper and the more recent *3:10 to Yuma* with Christian Bale. Even though cowboys are portrayed as free spirited and fun loving, if they committed to doing something, they did it.

As I grew up, I can remember my father saying things like "A promise made is a debt unpaid," or "Your word is your bond." And I can honestly say I remember few, if any, promises my father made to me, or others, that he broke. I can remember a time or two when he made a promise, and I'm sure he wished he hadn't. But "he was a man of his word." Today we would say, "Person of their word." Women also keep their word. Incidentally, he also expected others to keep their word. If they didn't, he would say that they weren't a gentleman. I learned when my father said someone wasn't a gentleman that was the worst insult he could cast on them.

As a young, adult sports fan, I can remember a professional football player who wanted to renegotiate his contract because someone else on the team had signed one for more money. I thought, *Wait a minute. He, along with his lawyer and agent, agreed on this five-year contract. Now, just because someone else got a better one, he wants to go back on his word?* That, incidentally, began my era of disillusionment with professional sports.

But then, that was another time. Today, wanting to renegotiate or just outright ignoring a promise is often the standard, even for our government.

Understand that keeping your word is more than just fulfilling a promise. Keeping your word is a vital part of who you are as a person. It's a part of your character. Without trustworthiness, agreements and promises, whether on paper or verbal, mean nothing.

I'm not a purest in that I believe all agreements can be done with the shake of a hand. Business arrangements are complicated, and honest misunderstandings do happen. I'm also not against lawyers. Most of us are not astute when it comes to complicated business and legal practices. So we need help to make sure when we sign on the dotted line, we've agreed to something we understand and can live up to.

But the vast majority of commitments we make aren't the type that requires a lawyer and a contract. These are the ones we most often break. "I'll take care of that" or "Don't worry. I'll go by and pick it up" is the type of commitment we most often break. A saying by an unknown author is very appropriate here: "Promises are like babies: easy to make, hard to deliver."

> "Promises are like babies: easy to make, hard to deliver."

We'll take a look at the pitfalls of not keeping our word and some methods of making sure either we don't make a commitment, or if we do, we keep the commitment.

Benjamin Franklin said a famous line—the last part of which we've all repeated on numerous occasions—"Our new Constitution is now established and has an appearance that promises permanency, but in this world, nothing can be said to be certain, except death and taxes."

I would love to say we can add "Keeping our word" to "death and taxes," but unfortunately or maybe even fortunately, we're all human and prone to mistakes. So we'll also examine how we approach someone when we've made a commitment that we find we can't fulfill.

But first, let's look at what happens when we don't keep our word.

The Pitfalls of Not Keeping Our Word.

It seems the people who habitually don't keep their word live in some kind of a daze. They've gotten to the point where letting someone down is normal. In the first place, they seem to feel it requires no apology, and if they're called on the carpet, they're the one who's offended because no one understands the situation. People do understand the situation. The situation is that the person who habitually fails to fulfill a promise is conceited and self-centered and doesn't give a darn about others. So what follows is . . .

1. You're Not Trusted

To put it simply, "A man or woman without their word is nothing." Trust is the glue that makes relationships work.

In this twenty-first century, things happen at an unbelievable speed. We travel down an interstate highway at seventy miles per hour and think nothing of it. There was a time in the late 1800s when people were concerned if vehicles traveled at that speed, the breath would be drawn from the passenger's lungs.

Computers, once occupying an entire room, now are the size of a briefcase—actually, even smaller than a briefcase, and they operate at a speed that ten years ago would have been unthinkable. Incidentally, a child's inexpensive computer has more memory and speed than the computer that took the first man to the moon and brought him back.

Yet when it comes to the speed in which we humans interact, because of the lack of trust, it makes contracts, documentation, and verification a necessity before people come to a simple agreement.

We've all experienced being told something, and during the process, even though the story was perfectly logical, we found we didn't believe what we were told. As we listened to the story and analyzed it on the conscious level, we were also receiving messages on the subconscious level. Eyes not meeting ours, a slight hesitation of the voice, and uncharacteristic body movements gave us the feeling something was wrong.

Although there are sociopathic people who have the ability to, as the saying goes, "Lie with a straight face," even these people aren't able to fool us very long.

Well-known lawyer Jerry Spence, responding to the question on how he's able to win all his cases, says, "There is a biological advantage to honesty. When you tell the truth, people can sense it. They trust you. If you compromise your integrity, you can't win their trust or your case."

I have an acquaintance; he would be considered a friend but for one flaw. He is the nicest person, a good husband and father, and a hardworking person. He's in an industry similar to mine, and when we first met, we would talk about business strategies that were beneficial to both of us. He would commit to e-mailing me the necessary information. Then I wouldn't hear from him for the longest time. He would literally disappear from my life. Fortunately, none of the things he promised was crucial. Now when we talk, and he says, "I need to get you . . ." I just say, "Great" and expect nothing to happen, and it doesn't. I just don't trust him.

Incidentally, if we don't have friends or can't keep friends, it might just be that a lack of trust is one of the major factors why people don't want to be around us.

> "Always keep your word; a gentleman never insults anyone intentionally; and don't look for trouble, but if you get into a fight, make sure you win."
> —Advice given to John Wayne by his father.

A Promise Is a Promise, Is a Promise

"He should have known I wasn't going to do that." "I agreed to do it just to get him off my back. It's not my fault. He shouldn't have been so pushy." "Everyone else was volunteering. I just got swept up in the excitement." Have you ever heard someone say that? Or maybe even said it yourself.

We tend to agree to something because we're wrapped up in the excitement of the moment, or we want to be seen as a "good guy." We always need to remember, no matter what our motivation, a promise is a promise, is a promise. And when we make a promise, we should try to deliver even more than we promise.

Does it matter if we break our word only once in a while? Actually, it does matter. It's like that leak under your bathroom sink. It starts with one drip—the drip symbolizing both the broken promise and the person breaking the promise. The water begins dripping regularly, and if it is allowed to go unchecked, soon we have a spurt and eventually a gusher.

John-Roger and Peter McWilliams, in their book *Life 101*, have come up with four categories of people who break promises. I wonder where each of us fits?

1. Rebels—These people say, "Rules are for fools." They're above all rules, and keeping a promise is a rule. But somehow, originally making the promise didn't involve rules.
2. Unconscious people—When a promise is broken, unconscious people's excuse is "I forgot." And they're astonished when it isn't sufficient. They come back with "You just don't understand. I wanted to do it. I just forgot. It's not my fault."
3. Comfort junkies—They agree to a promise if it's too uncomfortable not to agree. This usually happens when everyone else is agreeing. If they find they can't do something, they don't tell anyone because to tell the person affected is just too uncomfortable.

4. Approval seekers—Approval seekers are over-schedulers. When they can't fulfill a promise, it's because they were busy filling a promise for someone else.

Our word is one of the most precious things we own. It should never be given lightly.

1. Promises to Friends And Family

When we don't fulfill a promise made to friends and family, we have something going for us that we normally don't have in a business situation and never have with strangers. That something is a bank account.

By that I mean, if you've been a good friend, father, or mother, you've built up some credit with friends and children. It's a little like monopoly. When you land in jail, if you have the credits (cash), you can bail yourself out of jail.

Friends tend to forgive and forget a bit easier than spouses or children. After all, a friend can avoid us until the anger has blown over.

Surveys have shown that dependability always shows up in the top qualities people look for in a spouse. Understand when we don't fulfill a promise, we're hurting our marriage.

Keeping our promises reinforces the trust our spouse has in us. Not keeping our word says we just don't care.

And if our spouse thinks we don't care, that bank account is quickly depleted. If our spouse feels we don't care, he/she might just bug out taking our other bank account with them.

Also, understand children may not have the same status as adults and are under a parent's authority; keeping a promise to them is just as important as to an adult because we're teaching them how to conduct the rest of their life.

A father lifted his small son onto a tree branch in his backyard. The young boy wasn't comfortable at all and wanted to be taken down. Holding his arms out in a cradle, the father said, "The only way you'll get down is to jump. And I'll catch you." The boy hesitated. Again the father said, "Don't be a scaredy cat. Jump. I'll catch you."

So the son hesitantly leaned forward and pushed himself off the limb. Just as the boy got to the father, he pulled his arms away, and the boy fell to the ground. The young boy started crying, more from emotional than physical hurt.

The father said, "Let that be a lesson to you. Never trust anyone."

I hope no one would be harsh enough to treat his/her child this way. But how many times do we break our promises to our children? A promise to go out to a pizza joint for dinner can be as important to a child as two adults signing a million-dollar contract. I'm sorry you discovered there's a great basketball game on TV, and you want to watch the game instead of going out to get pizza. Your example is more important.

How many times have we seen or experienced a child being persistent? "But, Dad, can I go? Everyone's going. I really want to go." And on and on and on. Finally, just to shut up the kid, we say, "We'll see."

To a kid, "We'll see" is just a quarter of an inch away from "OK." We parents know we're going to have to address the problem later. But at least things are under control now.

A few years ago, a friend told me about an experience he had when in college. One of his fraternity brothers was a bartender in a nearby beer bar. This became the "after hours" meeting place for the party-loving fraternity brothers. One evening, one of the guys brought in a small frog he had found in the parking lot. In no time, they started betting on how far the frog would jump and in which direction. After a couple more beers, one of the guys said, "For $20, I'll eat that frog." Within minutes, twenty dollars was on the bar. The guy picked up the frog and said, "I guess if I have to eat the frog, I'm going to get it over with." He popped it in his mouth. Later, he said it was a bit bitter.

"Dang! I know what I promised...but I didn't think it would be so big!"

From that story, I came up with a bit of homespun philosophy. Any time I have to face something unpleasant (eat a frog), I get it done as quickly as possible. Later in the book, I'll refer to this as "eating the frog."

So if we don't want our child to go somewhere or do something, why not just eat the frog and tell him or her no from the beginning. If you have to tell your child something the child doesn't want to hear, do it immediately and firmly.

Incidentally, if we say our child can't do something, and later, because of additional information, we see no problem in allowing him to do it; we can always change your mind and let the child go. I think they'll forgive you for changing your mind in this incident.

Children never know what to expect from parents who don't keep their word. It causes anxiety, which shows up as anger and frustration.

Parents who are dependable and trustworthy tend to be at ease, patient, and have a high level of self-control, and their children have a high level of self-confidence.

2. Business Promises

It seems we increasingly have a generation of business people who believe that failing to meet a commitment is perfectly OK. In some cases, it seems to be a business strategy.

I recently read about a program used by some new stockbrokers to get a solid customer base in a short period of time. The program begins by the new stockbroker assembling an e-mail list of 2,500 potential clients.

He then selects a stock that has volatility. He e-mails half of the potential customers that the stock will go down and the other half that the stock will go up. Whichever the stock does, he now has 1,250 people, who are paying attention to his recommendations.

He does it again with another stock. Now he has 625 people, who are interested in his recommendations. After he does it two more times, he has 155 people, who are sure he's a genius and are a client base who will follow his every recommendation.

The bad news is there are people who have no integrity in every line of business. Fortunately, the vast majority of businesspeople are people of integrity, who keep their word. The challenge is finding them and avoiding the others.

Incidentally, being a person of your word also implies integrity. Businesspeople who practice integrity in their dealings find it saves rather than costs money.

We're all familiar with Wal-Mart. We should also be familiar with Warren Buffett and his company Berkshire Hathaway. A few years ago, Wal-Mart wanted to buy one of Warren Buffett's companies by the name of McLane Distribution. McLane Distribution had annual revenues of $23 billion.

Both companies wanted the deal to happen, and the basic agreement was hammered out in a two-hour meeting. Because both companies are public, there was other due diligence required. It's not unusual for a business transaction of this size to take up to a year to complete. But according to Warren Buffett, he trusted Wal-Mart, and he trusted the people on his team. Obviously, the Wal-Mart people did the same. The deal was closed in twenty-nine days.

Just think of the savings in legal and accounting fees, not to say anything about the salaries and time of the negotiators.

Without a doubt, business promises are most often broken when it comes to service.

I know we can all recite a litany of stories where promises were made and never delivered. Some were business to business, while others were promises made to us as a retail consumer.

It seems there is an extremely large percentage of business people who believe failing to meet a commitment is acceptable and possibly even a business strategy. I can assure you, it isn't.

Although we probably don't set out to develop a business plan to promise the customer anything just to get the order, many business owners and managers, as a result of laziness and low ethics, drift into this business model.

How many times have you heard a commercial on TV promoting a product with a "lifetime guarantee?" Sure, it's a lifetime, if you can track down the company that has changed its name and location shortly after the promotion ended. Or if they still are around when the product fails, you discover the product is replaced free, but shipping and handling cost more than the original product.

Bill Cosby once said, "The very first law in advertising is to avoid the concrete promise and cultivate the delightfully vague."

"Guaranteed satisfaction" is something often casually thrown around but seldom lived up to. I'm aware of a small company that has guaranteed satisfaction as a motto. It's not something they put on their literature or use in their advertising. It's just something they do. Sure, occasionally they run into an unreasonable customer. And every once in a while, they lose money on an order or even lose an order because of the demands of a customer. But they have an impeccable reputation. And I'm sure for every order they turn down because they can't meet the requirements of their potential customer, there are several others they receive as the result of satisfied customers telling their friends.

> "Character is what you are; reputation is what you try to make people think you are."

However, according to them, the greatest satisfaction they have is going to bed each night knowing they are people of character.

I don't know about you, but when I find a company with a great price, product, and service and it is possible to have all three, I'm excited, and I tell everyone I know about the company.

On the other hand, when I'm taken advantage of, everyone knows about that too.

The big box stores make it tough on small businesses. But they shouldn't. When I say that, I'm not in anyway saying we should do away with the box stores. They have every right to put one up anywhere they feel there is a sufficient customer base.

What I'm saying is I know many a small business that wasn't affected when a box store came into the area. Why? They provided a superior product and customer service that the box stores couldn't match.

How often have we walked into a small business to have the clerk or owner behind the counter taking care of some legitimate business, not looking up or speaking. After we look around the store, we leave wondering how they can stay in business.

No matter how hard they try, every business goofs up now and then. Sometimes, it's something that could be controlled, and other times, it's beyond everyone's control. Even though a customer might not act like it, everyone knows it happens. What makes a bad situation even worse is trying to crawfish out of it. It's time to eat the frog. If the solution is simple, correct it, and simply say you're sorry. If it's something major, admit the problem, explain what happened—that's not the same as making excuses—and ask the customer how it can be made right.

Everyone has been on both sides of the desk, and the vast majority of people are reasonable.

Some guidelines for staying out of trouble include the following:

- Don't promise anything you don't feel confident about delivering.
- Always keep in mind the implications of your promise.
- If it's something you don't normally do, make sure you've made a note of the commitment. Many times, commitments aren't followed through because they're forgotten.
- If unforeseen circumstances make it impossible to fulfill the commitment, notify the customer immediately. Eat the frog.
- If the commitment is unique, make sure your superiors are aware of it before the final handshake.

According to Harold Geneen, "It is an immutable law in business that words are words, explanations are explanations, promises are promises but only performance is reality." The bottom line in business is the same as in our personal life; doing what we say we'll do is not only the courteous way to do business, it's the only way.

3. Casual Promises

We've all heard of "little white lies." Not keeping a casual promise might be similar to a white lie.

Remember that social situation last week when someone you just met says, "You need to stop by sometime."

You responded, "Sure, I'll give you a call the next time I'm in the area. You do the same when you're in my area."

The whole time both of you know it won't happen. The exchange was purely social courtesy.

It's the same thing when we're invited to an event, and we respond, "I'll think about it." The chances are 99.5 percent that you're not going to be there.

Unfortunately, a casual promise is often like a white lie in that at the beginning, the white lie is as white as virgin snow. Later, it starts looking like two-day-old snow at the side of the road, and eventually, it's like that yuck piled up in a parking lot throughout the winter. I know anyone who lives in the south doesn't understand my visual illustration. Just take it from me; this is snow you wouldn't want your kids to play in.

Casual promises can be innocent. But always do a check with yourself to make sure no one is actually depending on your fulfilling it. Remember hurricanes and earthquakes get more news, but termites make more damage.

What's Needed to Keep Your Promise?

We don't have to worry about our keeping a promise that has a high level of benefit to ourselves. I'm not concerned about a person promising to cash a $1,000 check they have just been gifted. However, "I'll promise to send you a check tomorrow for that past-due bill" is another thing.

To keep a promise, we may regret giving takes a little extra in each of us. It takes the following.

1. Belief in Yourself

Just what does believing in yourself have to do with our keeping our word? Having a belief in yourself as a good person is that inner spark that starts the fire of determination.

OK, so it's hard to believe in yourself if you have a history of not keeping your word. One of the few things that I regret doing as a father raising two boys is telling them they were bad when they did something wrong. I'm not saying correcting a child will hurt a child. But what I should have said is "What you did is wrong. And you are too good a person to be doing such a thing." Incidentally, my boys had enough belief in themselves to overcome this error.

God has made each of us, and He doesn't make mistakes. The very fact we're alive means we're a worthy person. Just because we have a propensity for not following through on our commitments means what we do is bad, not that we are bad.

The best way of counteracting a lack of belief in ourselves is to take the same action we do in the morning when we're getting ready to take a shower. In the same way, we rob the hot water of its burning power by turning on the cold water; we need to immerse ourselves with a belief that no matter how many promises we've broken in the past, we have the ability to change.

> "No matter how many promises we've broken in the past, we have the ability to change."

2. Having Pride In Yourself

The book of Proverbs in the Bible says, "Pride goes before a fall." Therefore, we're admonished not to have pride. My belief is that the word *pride* is interpreted incorrectly. A more accurate translation would be "Conceit goes before a fall."

One of the things my father instilled in me from early childhood was to have pride in who I was and what I did. Each of us should have enough pride in who we are that we will become absolutely determined to keep our word.

So now we're determined. Just how do we actually change from undependable to dependable? Below are the steps.

How to Keep Your Word?

Hopefully, at this point, each of us has decided to become a person of our word, and we believe we have the ability to change. But how? Below are eight steps that will put us in the winner's circle.

1. Make A Commitment to Yourself

Before we make that first commitment to someone else, we need to make a commitment to ourselves. And that commitment is to honor any commitment we make to another person.

Over the years, I've read a number of books that have told me it takes twenty-one days to develop a new habit. That may very well be true, but it has always taken longer than twenty-one days for me unless it's a bad habit, that is.

In any event, whether it's twenty-one days or 210 days, that first step toward change is saying to ourselves that we're going to change and that change is for the good.

I'm not a pilot, but I have flown as a passenger more than my share of times. I'm told that when a plane flies from Los Angeles to Hawaii, it is actually off course some ninety percent of the time. Wind and other effects cause it to veer a bit. When it gets off course, the pilot doesn't yell at the plane or hit it with his fist. He doesn't give up and return to Los Angeles. He understands adjustments are necessary. And so the changes are made. And amazingly, at or near the appointed time, the plane arrives at the Honolulu International Airport.

I can assure you, and if you have the intelligence I believe you have, you already know that making a commitment to be a person of your word today will not put you on a course with no deviation.

It would be wonderful if we totally understand we will be periodically getting off course, and when we do, like a pilot, we calmly get ourselves back on course. Yes, it would be wonderful. However, if you're anything like me, when you goof up, you kick yourself from here to the North Pole.

So we need to not only commit to ourselves to begin a life of honoring commitments, we need to understand there will be failures. Therefore, we will additionally commit not to beat ourselves up when we get off course. We'll calmly say to ourselves, "I'm off course." We'll make the necessary adjustments, and then we'll continue on with a renewed enthusiasm.

Denis Waitley says, "Losers make promises they often break. Winners make commitments they always keep." I don't want the giant "L" on my forehead. What about you?

2. Think Before You Speak

Whether it's something as simple as telling our children we'll go to the show this weekend, a friend for whom we'll pick up an item the next time we're at the hardware store, or we'll give a lifetime guarantee on that product we just sold, we need to really mean it when we say it and not let our mouth overload our brain. Too often, we get ahead of ourselves and say things we shouldn't.

I know it may seem like bad manners to hesitate before we commit to something or even be audacious enough to ask to think about it before making a commitment. But I'll tell you, it isn't nearly as bad as jumping on the bandwagon, only to regret it later or even not follow through.

It's even more difficult when everyone around us is jumping on the bandwagon, and they're holding out their hands to pull us up there.

If we're just not sure we want to commit to something, it's OK to say something like "I'm just not sure I can do that. Let me check it out. I'll call you tomorrow to tell you for sure." And make sure you live up to the commitment to call them.

The interesting thing is, the ability to think about it not only gives us the opportunity to say no, when our initial inclination was to say yes, it also gives us the opportunity to say yes, when our initial inclination was to say no.

3. Don't Lie

It always intrigues me when a politician tells an out-and-out lie that even my ten-year-old grandson would know is a lie, fellow politicians, even on the other side of the aisle, hesitate to call the person a liar. They'll say, "He misspoke," "What he said wasn't accurate," or "He overestimated or underestimated the situation," but they'll never use the word "liar" because "liar" is a fightin' word.

I'm going to use it because it is a harsh word. And if we associate some of our actions with that word, maybe we'll change our actions.

I believe in black and white, but at the same time, I have a bit of a problem with absolutes. I learned a while back not to use the words "always" or "never" in conjunction with things I do because it seems God often calls me on my absolutes. I also have a problem with what people associate with total honesty. Unfortunately, total honesty is sometimes used as an excuse for offending people.

We've all known people who seem to take joy in exhibiting their honesty by volunteering comments like "Boy, that sure is an ugly shirt" or "Did you forget to put on makeup this morning?"

If we express any indication of being offended, their response is "Hey, I'm just being honest." They're not being honest; they're being rude.

"Yes, my friends, I know what I promised last election...but *this* time I really mean it."

On the other hand, if you're asked, "What do you think of my shirt?" an honest and diplomatic response would be "I think you look better in your blue one."

As we have said before, a white lie is still a lie. And we'll find that when we make a habit of accepting our telling white lies, we'll soon discover that the white turns gray and eventually black.

Then there's the embarrassment of being caught in your lie. And it will happen.

There's the story of the man who called his boss saying he would not be at work because he had to attend his grandmother's funeral. When he returned to work the next day, his boss asked him if he believed in life after death.

"Well, yes," replied the employee. "Why do you ask?"

"I'm glad to hear that. Your grandmother showed up yesterday looking for you."

4. Only Make Commitments We Can Keep

Sounds simple, doesn't it? All you have to do is make sure you don't commit to anything that you can't carry out. To be sure, those who are most slow in making a promise are the most faithful in the performance of it.

Well, it isn't, especially if we fall into one of the categories I mentioned earlier in the chapter—rebels, unconscious, comfort junkies, or approval seekers.

There are times when we look at something and say, "I have the skills to do it and the time, and I truly believe it should be done." So with little thought, we feel comfortable in committing to an idea or chore.

There are other times when we're not so sure. This is where we can get caught in quicksand. We need to be honest with ourselves and the other person. Let the other person know our doubts, but tell him that we'll do our best. Also make sure he understands that we may need some extra help. And incidentally, make sure you do your best.

Also, keep in mind there will be times when we make all kinds of caveats up front and then we're not able to complete the project, there are going to be those who forget the caveats, so we will end up with egg on our face. It will happen. I guarantee it. If we don't think we can take the possible pain, don't commit to anything we're sure we can't fulfill.

For several years, I worked with volunteers in raising funding for a nonprofit organization. My job was to organize volunteers in different cities to put on special fund-raising events. Over a period of ten years, I worked with volunteers in several different states. One state, which shall remain nameless, the volunteers were very enthusiastic. I had no trouble getting people to volunteer for all the needed jobs. They asked the appropriate questions, and my initial reaction was that meeting the fund-raising goals would be a piece of cake.

I soon learned there were some who were sincere, but a large percentage of the people's enthusiasm and commitment was just momentary. I ended up spending a vast amount of time following up with the volunteers and taking care of things that weren't done.

Later, I was responsible for a different state. When I asked for a volunteer for a specific job, someone would always raise their hand and say something like "I'll take care of that." No flags were waved, and no bugles were blown; just I'll take care of that. And you know what; it was taken care of to perfection. The reason was that they only made commitments they could keep.

Think back on the commitments you not only fulfilled but fulfilled with relish. Chances are it was something for which you had a passion. You not only worked hard on the fulfillment, but you were a bit disappointed when it was complete. So maybe we ought to focus on making commitments, involving those things with which we have a passion.

Now, there are literally millions of worthwhile causes in the world. And most of these causes save lives and eliminate suffering. But there is no way we can have a passion for all of them or even a small fraction of them. So it's OK to acknowledge the validity and need for something and tell them that's not where our passion is. They will probably try to explain that their cause is much more worthwhile than yours because their cause is where their passion is located. Again, acknowledge the validity of their cause and remain true to your cause. Incidentally, you're permitted to feel a little guilty when you walk away.

Always remember, we may receive praise and adulation when we commit to something, not keeping our word quickly damages our reputation.

> "Not keeping our word quickly damages our reputation."

5. Be Consistent

People often misquote Ralph Waldo Emerson by saying, "Consistency is the hobgoblin of little minds." That is not what Emerson said. What he said was "A *foolish* consistency is the hobgoblin of little minds."

He never discussed what "foolish" versus "wise" consistency was, but he did make a qualification for his statement by mentioning "foolish consistency" specifically. Even though I'm not a poet or a particular fan of Emerson, I believe each of us has enough God-given sense to know when we're being foolishly consistent. One can consistently bang their head against the wall and expect their intelligence to improve. Stupidity is when someone repeatedly does the same thing and expects a different result.

But on the other hand, consistency does matter. You don't see star athletes who are outstanding in one game and a bust in the next. They're not around long enough to become stars.

In baseball, if someone gets a hit every third time at bat, they're considered an above average hitter. In life, keeping our word even half the time just doesn't make it. Our friends will cut us from their roster. On the other hand, constantly keeping our word will make us all stars in the eyes of our friends.

Staying with the analogy, no one can bat a thousand. There are going to be those isolated times when we can't keep our promise. We'll address that situation a little later in this chapter.

6. Work Hard to Fulfill Our Promise

Promises are like crying babies in church; they should be carried out at once.

If we make a promise to someone, the other person assumes it's a done deal. Therefore, we should do everything in our power to fulfill it. We should give it 100 percent of our effort. If we give a promise a half-hearted effort, the promise is DOA, dead on arrival. And even if we fulfill the promise, everyone will realize we did it begrudgingly. And sometimes, that's worse than not doing it at all.

The above is particularly true when it's the first time we've made the promise to the person or the group. For, it is true that first impressions count. We learn a lot about a person when we ask him for a favor.

Think back in your life. Remember, when you asked someone for a favor, the person responded, "Sure. I'll take care of that." And he did just that. He even called us to tell us it was done, and is there anything else he can do? Chances are that the person became a good friend in a short time.

7. Don't Make Excuses

This is going to be short and sweet. Excuses are like bellybuttons; everybody's got one. While at the time excuses may appear valid, they tend to continually show up. It seems a person who makes excuses never runs out of them.

Excuses tend to be causes that are blamed on other people or circumstances. If the reason you didn't run in that marathon was that you broke both of your legs a week before the run, that's an acceptable cause. If you didn't run in the marathon because your alarm clock didn't go off, that's an excuse.

Be a man or a woman. Unless your legs are broken, simply say, "I goofed up. I'm sorry. How can I make it up?" However, don't be surprised if the person says "Just, forget it!" or something much worse.

You may be called undependable. But you won't be called a wimp. One final word. Actually, it's six words! "Excuses and trust don't mix well."

> **"Excuses and trust don't mix well."**

8. Remember Your Promises

Sometimes I wonder if there is anything between my ears. Not that I think I'm dumb. But I have the proverbial problem of having someone tell me something and have it go in one ear and out the other.

As a result, I keep a small spiral notebook and pen in my back pocket. When someone tells me something or I have a thought, I pull it out and write it down. Incidentally, I've had times when I've had a thought, and by the time I get the notebook and the pen out, the thought is gone. But that's my problem.

If you're the least bit like me, when you agree to a promise, write it down, along with all the particulars as to when and how it is to be carried out. First, it will lower your anxiety level. You won't have to worry about remembering the details. And second, it will impress the daylights out of the person you're talking to. It will also lower his anxiety level. He'll know you're serious about fulfilling the promise.

Always remember, no matter how insignificant a promise may be to us, understand it's extremely important to the person to whom we make it. Beyond the significance of the person expecting us to fulfill our promise, by not fulfilling a promise we're saying that person isn't important and we don't respect them.

What If We Just Can't Keep Our Promise?

It's a fact of life that we're not going to be able to fulfill every promise. Things happen. So what do you do?

1. Be Honest

There are times when we get wrapped up in the heat of the moment and make a commitment that minutes later, we regret. Often, it's the "people pleaser" in each of us that causes us to do it.

When this happens, we should take full responsibility for the outcome of our actions. Immediately tell the person, "I just misspoke. I'm not going to be able to do that." Incidentally, I love that word "misspoke." It's a nonthreatening way of saying "I lied" or "goofed up."

It's also important that you're able to sincerely portray to the other person that you are disappointed because you couldn't keep your word.

"Here's that old frog again."

Then there are times when we make a commitment, and several days or even weeks later, we realize we're not going to be able to fulfill that commitment. Here's where that old frog you have to eat shows up again.

Incidentally, there are times when you don't think you can fulfill a promise; you "eat the frog," and then something happens that allows you to fulfill the promise; it will only make you look better in the eyes of the other person.

2. If You Can't Do It When You Said, When Can You Do It?

As we indicated above, there are going to be times when even the most conscientious person just can't fulfill a promise. We've all agreed—or at least we're considering agreeing—that as soon as we realize we can't fulfill the promise, we'll tell those people involved. However, our obligation doesn't necessarily end there. If there is the opportunity, we need to seriously consider telling the person when and under what circumstances we can fulfill the promise in the future, that is, if we really do want to fulfill the promise. And for sure, if we want to be known as a person who keeps his or her word, we don't want to blow it a second time.

3. Promises That Were Never Made

Someone has said that half the promises people say were never kept and were never actually made in the first place. And whoever that someone is knows his stuff. No matter how careful we are about making promises, there is going to be someone who says we made a commitment that we didn't. Sometimes, it's an honest mistake. They wanted you to commit so bad that they actually believe you did. Or maybe you weren't extremely clear about not being able to commit.

Then there are those who actually lie. Yes, people lie about something as holy as making a promise. Often, it's to cover their own failure at fulfilling a promise.

In either case, what do you do? First, don't make a big issue about it. Because when you do, everyone will think, "Me thinks he protests too much."

> "Me thinks he protests too much."

The simplest thing to do is to say "I'm sorry. I was not aware that I made that promise. Can you refresh my memory about how I came to make this promise?" During their telling of the story, you will have the opportunity to ask additional questions. By the end of their story, you should know whether they were mistaken about your making the promise or whether they're trying to cover their own rear end. Conclude by asking if there is anything you can do at this point.

Again, maintain your emotional control. That will keep you in the driver's seat. It will also help convince observers that you are the one in the right.

When Others Don't Keep Their Promise

Until now, we've only addressed our keeping our word to someone else. There are going to be times when someone makes a promise to us and they don't keep it. How do we react to them?

1. Maybe I'll Find Out. We'll See

We've all been hurt, irritated, or angered when a person, a product, or a company doesn't fulfill their promise. And I can guarantee that it will happen again tomorrow, next week, or next month. It's the age in which we live.

But this is no excuse for you and me not to "be a person of our word" and commit to fulfilling our promises. It's got to start somewhere.

OK, it's time for a little stark reality. Think back to the last few times someone or a business made a promise that wasn't fulfilled. I'll bet at the time the promise was made, you were a bit skeptical that it would be fulfilled.

I have a friend who, when he gets work done around his home, not only looks for the best deal, actually finds someone who will do the work for much less than anyone else. It just so happens the person doesn't have a contractor's license, needs payment up front to buy materials, and even has to borrow tools from my friend. Then when the contractor doesn't show up for several days and often even disappears when the job is half done with the advance, he can't figure why people are always taking advantage of him. He should have known better than to depend on someone who is shadier than an oak tree.

Also remember, as an old proverb says, "When a man repeats a promise again and again, he means to fail you." And the great philosopher Shirley MacLaine has said, "It is useless to hold a person to anything he says while he is in love, drunk, or running for office."

Sure, there are going to be times when you have every confidence a commitment will be fulfilled, and it isn't, but as stated before, normally, even if it's just a still quiet voice, you'll hear "I thought so."

120

When you're "sucker punched," be gracious. And commit to yourself you will never let that person put you in that position again. That is unless you truly feel it happened under unusual circumstances and the person is able to sincerely convince you that it will never happen again.

In Conclusion

Believe in the power of the promise. People can overlook or forgive a lot of things, but one thing people find it hard to forgive is not fulfilling a promise. So only make a promise when you're passionate about it, and believe you can fulfill it. If you do, you'll discover you're not only able to sleep better at night, people will come to trust you, and you'll have a lot more friends.

Remember, when everything is said and done, the only person who, you can guarantee, will be trustworthy and honest is you. And the great thing is if you are trustworthy and honest, the chances are you'll attract people of like character.

Chapter 7

Go the Distance

Several years ago, as we were putting together the "living the code" precepts, we knew we needed to include something about quitting. We toyed with phrases like "Don't quit," but they seemed so negative. And as we've said before, everywhere we go we're bombarded with negativity; we didn't want something as positive as "the code" to be negative. So rather than being negative and saying what not to do, we decided to encourage everyone by telling them what to do—go the distance.

What Success Isn't?

Success, as the world measures, is highly subjective, particularly when someone is looking at it in another person's life.

I can remember an acquaintance remarking to me how successful a friend of mine was. I responded in some nebulous way about his being very nice.

What the person didn't know was, because of a recent business reversal, his company was about to go bankrupt and his home was in foreclosure.

We all remember actors or entertainers who, to the outside world, are famous and successful, only to hear on the morning news that they have committed suicide.

Then you have that highly successful financier Bernie Madoff, a man who was successfully investing other people's money in order to make them a success. As we all know Madoff's success was actually his ability to run a ponzi scheme.

So I guess success isn't something that can be successfully observed.

A few years ago, I went on an outfitted hunting trip to Colorado. My guide was a married young man with two children. He worked as a hunting guide during the winter and a cowboy at a local ranch during the summer. He owned a few acres of land and was in the process of building a home on a pay-as-you-go basis.

I visited his home. It was a small, two-bedroom place. The roof was completed and shingled. The subfloor was in place. The walls were simply heavy plastic stretched over the stud framing. They heated their home with a wood stove.

Most people would not say this young man was successful but not him. He and his wife were extremely happy. So success isn't standardized.

Another thing must be observed about success. If in twenty years that young guide/cowboy and his family are still living in a home with subflooring and plastic for walls, I don't think he or anyone else would think him successful. So for someone to truly be successful, he must continually be updating those successes.

There's a saying that goes, "He who dies with the most toys wins." So is success a big car, boat, and home? These things could be the result of success, but they don't necessarily equal success.

Recently, I received one of those e-mails that are regularly circling the Internet. Whether it is a true story or not is immaterial, the message is the thing. I would like to share it with you.

A few years after they graduated, a group of college friends decided to get together for a mini reunion at the town of their alma mater. During the evening as they were sitting in their old college hangout talking, it seemed most everyone was disappointed with the way their life was going. Then one graduate suggested calling Professor Johnson to see if he could get together with them and give them some guidance because Professor Johnson had been helpful to many of them while they were struggling students. The call was made, and he invited them over for some hot chocolate.

When they arrived, the hot chocolate was on the stove, and an assortment of cups was on the kitchen counter. The cups were porcelain, glass, and crystal. Some were plain looking, and some were expensive. A couple even had chips in them.

After everyone had selected their cup and filled it with hot chocolate, the professor started speaking:

"I notice that all the nice-looking and expensive cups have been taken, leaving behind the plain and chipped ones.

"While it is normal for you to want only the best for yourselves, that's the source of your problems.

"The cup you're drinking from adds nothing to the quality of the hot chocolate. What each of you really wanted was hot chocolate. The cup was just necessary to hold the hot chocolate, yet each of you went for the best cups, and soon you began eyeing each other's cups.

"Now, friends, please consider this. Life is the hot chocolate. Your job, money, and position in society are the cup. The cup is just a tool to hold and contain life. The cup you have doesn't define nor does it change the quality of the life you're living. By concentrating only on the cup, we fail to enjoy the hot chocolate God has provided us.

"Always remember this: it's the hot chocolate that's important, not the cup. The happiest people don't have the best of everything. They just make the best of everything they have."

So success isn't things.

Now that we know what success isn't, just what is it?

What Success Is?

John Wooden retired as UCLA's basketball coach with a record of ten NCAA championships in twelve years. Seven of those championships were consecutive. John Wooden's success was his ability to motivate players to be successful. And to accomplish this, he came up with a simple definition for success. It is "Peace of mind can be attained only through the self-satisfaction in knowing that you made the effort to become the best you're capable of becoming."

The key phrase in that statement is "knowing that you made the effort."

Just what does that mean? You walk up to a two-hundred-pound dumbbell, reach

"Knowing that you made the effort . . ."

down, and do everything you can to lift it over your head, but you can't. Have you "made the effort?" No way! What you do is come up with a program where you start with a seventy-five-pound dumbbell and over a period of weeks or even months build up to the two hundred pounds.

Success is earned. We would all love to win the lottery. It's interesting to study the lives of major lottery winners. The money seldom brings happiness with it. And after a period of time, a significant percentage of the winners end up worse off than before that "lucky day."

A big reason for this is that buying a lottery ticket doesn't equate with the labor necessary to earn millions of dollars. And there is a feeling down deep that they don't deserve the money. Having to work for a dollar makes one appreciate that dollar a lot more. Isn't there a saying that goes something like this? "Easy come, easy go."

Although I'll be sharing a number of illustrations where people have gone the distance and, as a result, become wealthy or famous, my intent is not to say that wealth and fame is the mandatory outcome for going the distance. The young guide/cowboy above will probably never be rich or famous, but he was on track to being successful by fulfilling his dream for his life.

Your dream and success can be anything that is legal and ethical as long as it makes you and your loved ones happy. Now, the dream of being able to watch TV for eight hours a day does miss the ethical goal a bit, that is, unless you have a job for a national newspaper or TV network as a TV critic.

Quit Is a Four Letter Word

As I look back on my life, I see my number-one reason for failing at something I was accomplishing was my quitting before I had victory.

Sometimes, I quit because I no longer wanted to accomplish that goal. It happens. We change. A high school basketball star, who had his goal to be a professional basketball player when in college, realizes he would rather be a doctor and becomes one. I wouldn't call him a quitter.

The majority of the time people don't follow through on a goal is because their objective wasn't as easy as they thought.

I'm reminded of that ditty we said as children. "A winner never quits, and a quitter never wins."

So if my goal is to win the Olympic gold metal in the hundred-meter dash and I end up with a silver metal, am I a quitter? As a total aside, a silver metal winner has a higher level of remorse about not winning the gold metal than a bronze metal winner. The silver metal winner is thinking, *If I had tried a little harder maybe I would have gotten the gold metal.* The bronze winner is just happy to be on the podium. Now, getting back to whether the silver metal winner is a quitter. Maybe at the moment he sees the result of the race, he may think so, but he sure isn't.

As we look at going the distance, we need to understand that in the same way it's impossible to fail completely, it's impossible to succeed completely. Even the gold metal winner may not have succeeded completely in his goal. He may have wanted not only to win a gold metal, but to set a world record.

At the same time, even though *quit* should be considered one of those bad four letter words, and during this chapter, we'll blame everything bad on it, a person who has tried and failed is a step above the person who never tries. At least, the person who tried has had the courage to try something different. They've been successful in making a commitment to something. They've been successful at discovering a way not to do something. As we shall see later, Thomas Edison was particularly successful at discovering ways not to do things."

President Theodore Roosevelt put it another way: "It is not the critic who counts, not the man who points out how the strong man stumbles, or where the doer of deeds could have done them better. The credit belongs to the man who is actively in the arena; whose face is marred by the dust and sweat and blood; who strives valiantly; who errs and comes up short again and again; who knows the great enthusiasm and the great devotion and spends himself in a worthy cause; who, at the worst, if he fails, at least fails while daring

> "The world is divided into people who do things and people who get the credit; try to belong to the first class—there's far less competition."

greatly so that his place shall never be with those cold and timid souls who know neither victory nor defeat."

It's better to try something and fail than to attempt nothing and succeed. But the object of this chapter is not just to motivate each of us to attempt something but to show us how to be successful in our attempts.

People Don't Fail, They Quit

Let's be blunt. Getting in the habit of quitting is one of the fastest ways possible of screwing up our lives. And we continue quitting simply because it's so easy.

Although it may be subtle, there is a difference between failing and quitting. A bridge that collapses, an electric frying pan that no longer heats up, and a battery that won't turn over a car's engine have all failed. They are all inanimate objects, and so unlike us, they don't have the ability to choose to no longer operate properly.

On the other hand, we as humans have the ability to make decisions and choices. Although a part of our physical body may fail, it doesn't mean we should quit. Incidentally, we've all read or seen stories of men and women with unbelievable physical handicaps succeeding in marvelous ways.

One of these people is Kyle Maynard. Kyle was born with congenital amputation. That means he has short stubs for arms and legs. Yet Kyle wanted to live his life as normal as possible. He went to public school. In high school, he decided he wanted to go out for the wrestling team. Fortunately, he had a coach who was willing to work with him.

During his freshman, sophomore, and junior years, he lost virtually all his matches. By his senior year, he had developed a wrestling style that was virtually unbeatable. Today, Kyle Maynard is a highly successful owner of a health club. Incidentally, if you want to read his story, he's written an autobiography entitled *No Excuses*.

When I hear one of these stories, my first reaction is to admire the person's drive and determination. My second reaction is to say to myself, "You stupid idiot, you have two legs and two arms. You can see and hear. You should be able to do ten times more than you do." Yes, I am my own worse critic.

Be Courageous

Everyone goes through times of doubt and fear. Even great and famous people have their doubts and fears. Fernando Espuelas, in his book *Life in Action*, tells about two such people.

We're all familiar with the strength and determination exhibited by Winston Churchill during World War II. Were it not for him, England would surly have been defeated, and possibly the war itself would have turned out differently.

What people then, and even now, don't know is that Prime Minister Churchill suffered from acute depression. He named it "the black dog." The black dog was a lifelong battle with depression, fear, and self-doubt. It was so severe that he would be bed ridden for days at a time.

Another great man—probably our greatest president—suffered all his life with depression, anxiety attacks, and nightmares. Before he became president, his friends would often keep him under a suicide watch. That president's name? Abraham Lincoln.

According to Espuelas, these men were able to deal with their depression and anxiety because they devoted themselves 100 percent to a great cause.

Their "great cause" was the survival of their country. However, a great cause doesn't have to be that "great." It can be something as simple as being the best person we can be. And let me tell you, being the best person you can be could very well accomplish things that are as important as what Churchill and Lincoln accomplished.

> "Courage is the mastery of fear, not the absence of fear.
> —Mark Twain"

Espuelas says, "Everyone knows fear. Everyone doubts his or her talents and vision sometimes. Successful people find a way to get around those doubts and persevere."

Wrong Thoughts About Success

1. Successful People Are Lucky

"Some people are just lucky." How many times have you heard someone say that or even said it yourself? I know I've said it a time or two.

At one time, we went to a church where the minister didn't believe in luck. When we had what most churches call "pot luck," he called it pot providence. Even William Shakespeare got in on the luck thing by saying, "Fortune brings in some boats that are not steered." I've heard many times that "luck is preparation meeting opportunity."

I looked it up in a dictionary and got this: "Luck or fortuity is good or bad fortune in life caused by accident or change and attributed by some to reasons of faith or superstition, which happens beyond a person's control." Sometimes, I think a dictionary could make the word *pizzazz* boring. On the other hand, recently when I had lunch in a Chinese restaurant, I got a fortune cookie with the following fortune: "Luck is the by-product of busting your fanny." Now, that's pizzazz.

The belief that some people are lucky and other people are unlucky takes success and failure out of our hands and puts it in the hands of fate. In addition, we develop animosity and envy toward those we feel are more fortunate than us.

When an injustice, either real or perceived, comes our way, it's easy to become resentful. Sometime during our life, all of us have harbored resentment. We've done it because we wanted to make our failure palatable by explaining it in terms of unjust treatment by others. "If we were treated the same way . . . If we got the same breaks . . ." "If they weren't the bosses' pet . . ."

Resentment is a cure, worse than the disease of being treated unfairly. Resentment, even when based on a real wrong, can be a habit. A bad habit. As long as we harbor resentment, it's impossible for us to look upon ourselves as a self-reliant, independent person. People who harbor resentment turn over their lives to other people.

I believe there are times when, out of the blue, some good fortune comes our way. As the saying goes, "Even a blind hog gets an acorn now and then."

But what about those people who seem to have all the luck? We all have opportunities come our way. For some of us, they're like ships passing in the night. We may even make the comment about how the thought we just had or idea someone mentions to us was interesting, but that game on TV was more interesting. Lucky people will notice the opportunity and act upon it. They have developed their intuition to the point that they will use it to make a decision. And they expect the best when they make a decision.

But all luck isn't good luck. Sometimes you're handed a lemon. What do you do? Well, some people make lemonade out of it.

Although you don't hear about it that much anymore, Ivory soap was a mistake. When a batch of soap was made, the machine mixing the soap was left on too long and an extra amount of air was mixed into the batch. Fortunately, before it was thrown out, someone realized the extra air in the soap made it float. Thus a new product was invented.

We all use "post-it notes." This indispensable product came from a mistake. It also illustrates how "luck" has little to do with success. It's persistence. It also has the elements of noticing an opportunity and acting upon it that we talked about above.

By accident, in 1968, Dr. Spencer Silver, a chemist at 3M in the United States, developed a "low-tack," pressure sensitive adhesive. For five years, Silver promoted his invention within 3M, both informally and through seminars, but without success. In 1974, Art Fry, a colleague of his came up with the idea of using the adhesive to temporarily anchor a piece of paper to another piece of paper.

In 1977, a product was developed and marketed under the name of Press 'N Peel. It went nowhere and was about to be dropped when, in 1978, free samples were given to people in Boise, Idaho. Ninety-five percent of the people said they would buy the product. It was reissued under the name of "Post-It Notes" aided with a large advertising campaign. As they say, "the rest is history."

These aren't the only products that came about as a result of mistakes. So did insulin, penicillin, quinine, and X-rays.

The people who invented these items had to overcome business hurdles to become successful. Their hurdles are nothing compared to the story of W. Mitchell we talked about in Chapter #4.

As a result of two accidents, Mr. Mitchell has burn scars over 65 percent of his body, no fingers on his hands, and is permanently paralyzed from his waist down. Even with these handicaps, W. Mitchell became a millionaire businessperson and the mayor of his hometown, flies his own plane, and is a much sought-after public speaker. Why? It's because of his attitude.

According to W. Mitchell, "Before I was paralyzed, there were ten thousand things I could do. Now there are nine thousand. I can either dwell on the thousand I lost or focus on the nine thousand I have left. I tell people that I have had two big bumps in my life. If I have chosen not to use them as an excuse to quit, then maybe some of the experiences you are having which are pulling you back can be put into a new perspective. You can step back, take a wider view, and have a chance to say, 'Maybe that isn't such a big deal after all.'"

Persistance and courage aren't character traits most people are born with. They are learned through persistance and courage. We can't eliminate fear. A hero isn't a person without fear. He has as much fear as anyone else. The difference between a hero and a coward is that the hero does his duty in spite of the fear.

"It's not what happens to you, it's what you do about it."

"Remember, it's not what happens to you, it's what you do about it."

2. Successful People Don't Fail

When we see or read about someone who has suddenly become successful in sports, arts, or business, we have the tendency to think them lucky (see above for "luck") or extremely talented and therefore they became a success overnight. Not so. Successful people fail a lot more than people who are failures.

Anyone who knows the history of baseball is familiar with Babe Ruth and his home run records. But did you know he also held strikeout records?

Did you know that Thomas Edison has been called the greatest failure in the history of invention? He failed more times and lost more money in unsuccessful experiments than any other inventor in modern history.

Edison failed ten thousand times while trying to develop the electric light bulb. He failed over seventeen thousand times while attempting to develop latex, the basis for our modern rubber industry.

At the same time, Thomas Edison was the greatest inventor in modern history. When he died, he held 1,097 patents.

Charlie Brown remains one of my more favorite cartoon characters. It's in part because I understand the cartoons, and Charlie Brown was always more naive than I was. That gave me comfort.

Although Charles Schultz, the creator of the cartoon, has been dead for a number of years, Charlie Brown cartoons can still be seen in newspapers.

Not many people know that Charlie Brown was Charles Schultz's alter ego. Deep inside, Schultz said he was Charlie Brown. And Schultz could never understand why people thought Charlie Brown was a loser. Schultz always said that losers would give up, and Charlie Brown never gave up.

Everyone is a success. No matter what we attempt, we succeed. We always succeed at producing results. The results may not be what we have planned or intended. But at least, there are results. And those results can be valuable if they're looked at correctly.

We need to understand it's the exception when we try something new and have the outcome be exactly what we have hoped for.

If we fail in a colossal way, we have just created the opportunity to show outstanding future successes in that area. We also know we've experienced the worst.

If we succeed, but not at the level we had envisioned, we should congratulate ourselves for the success and analyze how improvements can be made.

If we succeed the first time we try something, the success would be meaningless. It's the rain that gives us the appreciation of the sun.

The Biosphere near Tucson, Arizona, has a complete community under a dome. There are large trees gorwing under that dome. Several years ago, the directors of the Biosphere noticed the trees were drooping.

After investigating, they discovered the trees were very weak. Why? Because there was no wind in the Biosphere. What does wind have to do with it? Well, it seems the wind that makes trees whip back and forth actually makes the trees stronger. And if there is no wind, the trees become weak and don't even have enough strength to be able to hold themselves up straight.

What does this mean to us? Quite possibily, the winds of strife we encounter actually make us stronger.

The fear of failure is the greatest single obstacle to anyone's success. The fact is success is impossible without first encountering failure. If you don't fail while going down the wrong path, how can you know you're on the wrong path?

One characteristic all super successful people have in common is the belief there is no such thing as failure. There are only results. It isn't that they don't fail. It's the attitude they have about failure. They look upon it as a learning experience. Life tends to repeat lessons over and over until we learn them. How do we know when we've learned a lesson? When we change our behavior.

Buckminster Fuller wrote, "Whatever humans have learned had to be learned as a consequence only of a trial and error experience. Humans have learned only through mistakes."

Could it be that the more times we fail at something, the greater our eventual success?

Keep in mind that everyone gets discouraged. A study of successful people shows that at some point, every one of them became discouraged; some quite often. At times, it seemed as if everything was going against them, and they wanted to quit. Or just as they experienced success, they encountered some personal tragedy. Yet they kept going and succeeded.

"The only time you mustn't fail is the last time you try."

A person can experience discouragement and continue working toward their goal. Shoma Morita said, "When running up a hill, it is all right to give up as many times as you wish, just as long as your feet keep moving."

3. People Are a Victim of Their Circumstances

One of the easiest and the most persistent excuses for being a failure is, "I'm the wrong color or I grew up on the wrong side of the tracks." There are those who are going to reply, "You don't understand. You're the right color, and you grew up on the right side of the tracks." And they're correct. No one can say that about the richest woman in the world, Oprah Winfrey. As a teenager, she had three strikes against her, but she refused to leave the batter's box. The rest is history.

Sadly, many decide the deck is stacked against them because of their race, sex, education, or physical handicap and they use that as an excuse for failure. It's interesting that successful people don't talk about their disadvantages as excuses. They talk about them as challenges they overcame on the way to success.

Everyone's circumstances are different, and people succeed in spite of or because of their circumstances. Read again the section about successful people failing.

I've read stories of people who were born into wealthy families and even families with title and who say no one understands the pressures on someone who has business and social pressures of the privileged.

It's not who you are or under what circumstances you live, but the tenacity of purpose that you have.

Here's a fact of life. Life isn't fair.

> **"Here's a fact of life. Life isn't fair."**

That's right. Life isn't fair. No matter how much the government or social organizations work at it, the playing field isn't level or will it ever be level. Once again, life isn't fair, and it never will be. And a realization of this can actually be liberating.

Accepting the fact that life isn't fair keeps us from feeling sorry for ourselves by allowing us to do the best with what we have. It also keeps us from feeling sorry for other people because we understand everyone is dealt a different hand.

This unfair life assures us of problems. And these problems are going to bring stress into our lives. At the same time, it's interesting to note the amount of stress we have over a problem is proportional to the way we relate to the problem. The more we rudiment over a problem and the more we struggle with a problem, the bigger it becomes, at least in our minds.

In the same vein as thinking a glass is half full, as opposed to half empty, looking at a problem as something that's an element of life and potentially a learning opportunity as opposed to a handicap and catastrophe takes away from the problem's impact.

I'm not a marshal arts expert, but I've been told by people that a successful takedown depends in part by a person's ability to use an opponent's momentum against him. To use the problem's momentum, one needs to ask himself or herself what lesson the problem can teach.

Because life isn't fair doesn't mean we shouldn't do everything in our power to do everything possible to accomplish our dreams.

Everyone has handicaps. Some are obvious; others aren't. I believe God has given us these handicaps so we will be challenged. I also believe He would not give us a handicap that we don't have the ability to overcome.

People may lack the desirable traits; they may have a score of weaknesses, but persistence, grit, and vision are always a part of a person who accomplishes things. This person will persist no matter what comes because persistence is a part of his nature.

Dave Thomas was the founder of the Wendy's fast-food chain. It's the number-three fast-food chain in the world.

Dave didn't start on the fast track to success. He never knew his real parents. He was adopted at the age of six weeks. He dropped out of school at fifteen. One of his first jobs was slinging hash for 35 cents an hour.

What made Dave Thomas different was a dream that he had since he was eight years old. That dream was to some day own the best restaurant in the world. Although there may be a lot of debate about Wendy's being the "best" restaurant, no one can question its being one of the most popular.

Although each of us starts out under different circumstances, it doesn't change the fact that we all started with the same opportunities in a free country. It's the opportunities, not the circumstances that make us different.

In addition, no matter what our circumstances, others have succeeded under the same and even worse circumstances.

4. Arguing for Your Limitations

How good are you at defending your beliefs? You're probably a lot better than you think.

How often have you said something like "I just can't do that" or "I just can't help doing that?" Maybe you say something like "I'm just not smart enough."

What you're doing is arguing for your belief. And the interesting thing is your ability to convince someone else is less important than your ability to convince yourself. Once you say "I'm not able to . . ." you start looking for examples to defend your belief.

Keep in mind, whatever you say after the word *I'm* defines you. If you say, "I'm always late," you're defining yourself as a person who's always late. If you say, "I'm a person who always works at being on time to appointments," you identify yourself as a person who values promptness.

Don't allow yourself to argue your limitations. It's a negative habit that with work can be overcome.

When we argue for our limitations, we usually find we're able to convince ourselves of those limitations, and those limitations become a fact of life. It's like putting a governor on an Indianapolis Speedway race car. It makes no difference of the car's potential; the governor won't allow the car to go faster than thirty miles per hour.

Maybe you do have some mental or physical limitations and can't do as much as the rest of us. That doesn't mean you're excused from doing anything.

A legend in the Middle East tells of a man who came across a sparrow lying on his back in the middle of the road. The man asked the sparrow what he was doing on his back in the middle of the road.

"I heard the heavens were going to fall today," responded the sparrow.

Laughing, the man asked, "I guess you think your spindly legs will hold up the heavens?"

"One does what one can," said the sparrow.

Not being able to do everything is no excuse for not doing all you can.

Correct Thoughts

1. Success Is Earned

We've all seen or even experienced success coming easily. The first time at bat, the batter hits a home run. On the first hunting trip, the young man bags a trophy animal. An executive is propelled into the president's office at a young age. As exciting as all these may be, when success comes easily, the successful person almost always questions whether the success is a fluke. He asks himself if he can continue the success. Can I write another hit song?

We're all familiar with the Beatles. Their songs are still played on the radio thousands of times each day. The Beatles were able to produce the string of hits because they had honed their skills through hundreds of performances. Many times, they performed more than once a day.

People flourish when they have to work for their success. And the great thing about living in a free country as we do is that people are able to earn their own success, which is necessary to live a fulfilled life.

Once again, let me remind everyone, money doesn't necessarily equal success. Too often, basing success on the amount of money we have is much like getting hooked on drugs. The more you have, the more you want.

When people are asked how much money they need to feel successful, they said about 40 percent more than they presently have. This was true of people making minimum wage as well as those making millions. Ben Franklin said that money doesn't fill vacuums, it makes vacuums.

In order to feel we have earned success, it's necessary to create value in our lives as well as other's lives. Earned success is what people create through passion, innovation, and hard work.

To that person who inherits a position or fortune, you can show you earned it by discovering ways your position or money can give opportunities for other people to be successful and flourish.

2. Success Comes from Hard Work, Not Just Hard Labor

According to the dictionary I keep in my bookcase, *work* is "physical or mental effort or activity directed toward the production or accomplishment of something."

I felt it was necessary to include this because there are some people who feel that work is physical labor, where the worker gets his hands dirty and sweats. This is surely work. And putting roofing on homes in a housing development in Phoenix, Arizona, in the summer is hard work.

At the same time, the executive who may spend his day in an air-conditioned office, figuring costs, finding suppliers, and negotiating with developers to get jobs is also working. It's just a different type of work. The dictionary defines work as "physical or mental."

As a person who has been on both sides of the desk, there are times when physical labor entails less tension and stress than mental labor.

But the great thing is, whether your success is the result of physical or mental labor, it is still success.

3. Persistence Can Overcome Skills, Talents, and Smarts

When I think of someone who's persistent, I always think of that great Paul Newman movie *Cool Hand Luke*. While a prisoner at a state work farm, Luke got in a fight with a bully fellow prisoner. Luke was totally outclassed. But every time he was knocked down, he got back up. Finally, out of frustration, the bully gave up. Luke won not because he was the toughest but because he refused to quit.

We've all seen TV commercials for 1-800-Flowers. The man with the week's growth of beard, who is the spokesperson for the company, is Jim McCann, the owner of the company.

As a young man, Jim had bought a small flower shop and was successful. Then he heard about a phone order flower company with the great name and phone number of 1-800-Flowers that was for sale. Coming up with every penny he had, Jim McCann bought the company. Today, he calls it, "the worst deal of his life and the best deal of his life." This is because after taking possession of the company, he discovered it was seven million dollars in debt. When he was able to scrape up enough money to get the phones turned back on, he discovered no one was calling in.

Now, that indebted company is one of the most successful businesses in the United States.

Jim says that he's a success because of sheer will and brawn, not superior intelligence. After all, he did buy a company deep in debt without knowing it. His final words on the subject are "Never give up."

The story is told of a mule that fell into an abandoned well. Even though the animal wasn't injured, the mule's owner couldn't get him out of the well. The owner decided the only thing he could do was to fill up the well. Although it would bury the live mule, it would make sure nothing else fell into the well.

At first, the mule became hysterical as the dirt fell on his back. Then he realized he could shake off the dirt and step on top of it. The mule kept shaking off the dirt and stepping up on top of the pile until he stepped out of the well.

Deep in that well, the mule, normally a strong defiant animal seemingly had no power. What he realized was that dirt with the power to bury him also had the potential to save him.

Most of us are familiar with the inspiring line from Winston Churchill's speech to his "old school" that he delivered on October 29, 1940. But that line, as inspiring as it is, wasn't the whole speech. Below isn't the whole speech either. But I believe it gives us a better picture of the determination needed to be able to overcome obstacles:

"You cannot tell from appearances how things will go. Sometimes imagination makes things out far worse than they are; yet without imagination not much can be done. Those people who are imaginative see many more dangers than perhaps exist, certainly many more than will happen, but then they must also pray to be given that extra courage to carry this far-reaching imagination.

"But for everyone, surely, what we have gone through in this period—I am addressing myself to the school—surely from this period of ten months, this is the lesson: never give in, never give in, never, never, never, never in nothing, great or small, large or petty—never give in except to convictions of honor and good sense. Never yield to force; never yield to the apparently overwhelming might of the enemy.

"Never, never, never give in."

We stood all alone a year ago, and to many countries, it seemed that our account was closed and we were finished. All this tradition of ours, our songs, and our school history and this part of the history of this country were gone and finished and liquidated.

"Very different is the mood today. Britain, other nations thought, had drawn a sponge across her slate. But instead, our country stood in the gap. There was no flinching and no thought of giving in, and by what seemed almost a miracle to those outside these islands, though we ourselves never doubted it, we now find ourselves in a position where I say that we can be sure that we have only to persevere to conquer."

"All things are possible."

If an obstacle in front of you seems impossible, always remember you can go around it, over it, or under it. A wise man once said, "All things are possible."

We need to say to ourselves, "I will not quit. I will keep on striving until I climb over, find a pass through, tunnel under, or stay and turn the mountain into a gold mine."

What Keeps Us from Success

There are three elements that are basic for every person's success. They are desire, belief, and expectation.

None of these elements are based in hope or wish. The dictionary defines *desire* as a longing or craving. *Belief* is the mental acceptance of, or conviction in the truth of, something. And *expectation* is considering something likely or certain.

These are strong words—words that drive people to accomplish great things, words that keep people going when faced with failure, words that when allowed to consume a person, inspire others.

Sometimes, we may have those elements in our life, yet we allow other, seemingly insignificant things to short circuit desire, belief, and expectation.

Let's take a look at some of these.

1. Bad Choices

It seems that some people are determined to make bad choices.

Incidentally, there is a difference between bad choices and wrong choices. A wrong choice is when a person analyzes a situation, and given the evidence at hand, they choose a course of action that fails—a bit like Thomas Edison did while inventing the light bulb.

A bad choice is when a person chooses to drive fifty miles per hour in a thirty-mile-per-hour zone. A bad choice is charging $3,000 on a credit card at 23 percent interest for a wide-screen television because the person knew he would enjoy the Super Bowl much better on the wide-screen than on his old television.

More often than not, bad choices come from the spoiled child within us. "I don't care what the rules are. I want it now."

Recently, I was getting my hair cut by a female barber. OK, so she was a beautician. Although I hardly knew her, she started telling me about how her third marriage was failing. It seems she's a party person, but none of her husbands ever wanted to go anywhere or do anything.

On top of that, they never seemed to have a job, and she had to be the breadwinner.

She made a bad choice, not once, but three times. Incidentally, if after she gets rid of this husband and she finds another, he will be the same as the first three.

Edison may have failed ten thousand times, but I can guarantee he didn't try the same experiment a thousand times.

Someone had said craziness is doing the same thing and expecting different results.

Bad choices tend to be repetitive. So if you find the same or even a similar problem keeps popping up in your life, you may be making bad choices in that area.

Bad things happen in everyone's life. But there is no reason for helping them along by making bad decisions.

2. Taking No for an Answer

According to Stephen Covey, "Opposition is a natural part of life. Just as we develop our physical muscles through overcoming opposition, such as lifting weights, we develop our character muscles by overcoming challenges and adversity."

"Opposition is a natural part of life."

Everyone faces opposition—the richest of us as well as the poorest and the most talented as well as Mr. "No Talent" himself. And as Stephen Covey indicates, the way we develop the skills to be successful is to overcome that opposition.

When I started in sales as a young man, I was told that sales is a numbers game. The more companies you call on, the more sales you make. And each time you get rejected, you're one step closer to a sale. The problem is it's not as simple as pulling the handle on a slot machine. The analogy being the more times you pull the handle of a slot machine, the more likely you are to hit the jackpot.

When you make a cold call on a potential customer, you're opening yourself to rejection. And nobody likes rejection. But to be successful, you have to be willing to take rejection over and over again. That's what every successful person has encountered over and over again. But they are fortunate enough to have enough confidence in themselves or their product to keep coming back again and again.

I've found some of my greatest successes have come after someone tells me no concerning something for which I have passion. There's something inside me that says, "Who does he think he is? I'll show him." And I find I become all the more determined.

I have a Hopi spirit doll called a kachina. Normally, these are made from a combination of painted wood, leather, and feathers. This one has been cut from a three-inch-thick piece of stone. The cuts are sharp and clean. It's unmistakable in the way it looks. This spirit doll was cut from the stone in a matter of minutes using a jet of water. There was nothing special about the water. It came from the same source the machine operator had used earlier to quench his thirst.

If a steady flow of water was continuously poured over the same stone, it would take years for it to wear through. The result would be a smooth, formless piece of rock.

This is the power of focus. The ability to focus on the outcome you desire has a power that's unmeasurable.

Shakespeare has said, "Is it not strange that desire should so many years outlive performance?"

Desire is the focus that creates unmistakable results.

If you truly have a goal that you are passionate about, don't allow anyone to dissuade you from achieving it. Virtually, every successful person you can think of has been in your situation. So why not join the successful crowd by not letting anyone keep you from going the distance.

In addition, always keep in mind that person who's an obstacle to your accomplishing your objective may just be yourself. You will never go beyond the obstacles you've put up in your own mind. If you think you can't do something, you never will because you've already lost the battle.

3. Not Taking Action

Recently, I was reading a book about how to be a survivor in different types of catastrophes. According to the author, the biggest difference between someone who survives and someone who doesn't survive is the person who dies doesn't take positive action during the accident.

He even says sometimes doing the wrong thing is better than doing nothing. And let me say, here procrastination is no action.

People who are paralyzed into inaction are normally in that condition because of a fear of failure. The interesting thing is when we don't take action, our lack of action results in failure.

I believe in God and that He wants the best for each of us. But no matter how much He wants the best for us, it's essential we take action that's for our benefit.

The story is told of a man whose house was in the way of an oncoming flood. Emergency people in a truck came by to help him evacuate his home. The man told the emergency people, "I'm going to stay. God will take care of me."

The flood came and required the man to go to the second floor of his home. A boat with some of his neighbors came by and begged him to come with them. Again he responded, "God will take care of me."

He finally had to retreat to the roof of his house. While on the roof, a helicopter dropped a rope ladder to rescue him. "God will take care of me," he said one last time.

The flood finally took his life. When he appeared before God, the man expressed his disappointment. "I had faith that You would rescue me. But You didn't."

God responded by saying, "I tried. Who do you think sent you the rescue truck, the boat, and the helicopter?"

"Even with God, action is required on our part."

Even with God, action is required on our part.

There is also that person who takes no action because they're afraid of succeeding. Now, that's a real catch-22. But why would we be afraid of succeeding. It puts us in the spotlight, and the pressure is on to perform successfully over and over again.

Each of us has a fear factor built inside us. That fear factor is good. It keeps us from walking down a dark alley at 2:00 a.m. The fear of starving, or getting fired, makes us get up each morning and go to work. Some fear is good. I have a friend who was in the Special Forces. He said those people who had no fear were usually the first to die in combat.

Fear can also keep us from realizing our best. When we don't do something because of the fear of failure or criticism, it very well could be good fear that has been misplaced.

144

A beggar, asking for money, approached a New York businessperson. Before the businessperson had a chance to say no, his eyes and the beggar's met. Through the beard, weathered face, and dirty clothes, the businessperson saw something familiar in the beggar's eyes.

"Don't I know you?" asked the businessperson.

"Yes, I'm a college classmate," responded the beggar.

After they talked for a while, the businessperson pulled out his checkbook and wrote a thousand-dollar check in the name of the beggar. "You take this check and use it to help get yourself a new start."

The beggar took the check and headed toward the nearest bank. As he stepped inside the bank, he noticed the opulence of the bank and the clothes of the customers and tellers, and decided because of his looks, they would believe he had stolen or forged the check. So he folded it, put it in his pocket, and walked back to the street. He never cashed the check.

Each of us has been given the resources to do great things. Many of us never use them because of assumptions and fears.

The story is told of a village with a wise old man the villagers would consult for advise.

One day, a farmer came to the wise man. "Help me," he cried. "My ox has died. And he was the only animal I had to help me work my fields. It's the worst thing that could happen to me!"

The wise man simply said, "Maybe so, maybe not."

The farmer went home disappointed that the wise man couldn't help him.

The next day, a young horse showed up on the farmer's land. The farmer caught the horse, and he found the horse could plow his field better than the ox. He was very happy and applolgized to the wise man for his earlier thoughts. The farmer said the death of his ox was the best thing that could have happened to him.

The wise man responded, "Maybe so, maybe not." The farmer went home, frustrated.

A few days later, the farmer's son was riding the horse. The horse bolted and bucked off the boy, breaking the boy's leg. Now the son couldn't help with the farming.

Again the farmer went to the wise man and asked him how he knew finding the horse wasn't a good thinig.

Again, the wise man merely said, "Maybe so, maybe not."

"If we don't start, we don't stand a chance of getting there."

Totally confused, the farmer once again returned home.

Less than a week later, it was announced that war had broken out, and every able-bodied young man had to go to war, and chances were most of them wouldn't return alive. Because of the son's injury, he didn't have to join the army.

The moral of the story? Even though we may think we know the significance of what happens to us, in truth, we only "think" we know.

Think of the times you thought an event was the end of the world. In retrospect, it wasn't. So as you encounter fearful events, remember the wise man of the village.

In reality, fear is our desire to arrive unscathed at the end of our life. And that isn't going to happen, no matter how hard we try. We need to accept those fears that prolong our lives and question those that keep us unscathed.

Scared stiff That's a very descriptive term. We've all been scared stiff during our lifetime. Normally, this happens when we encounter something that frightens us. At this time, our adrenaline starts pumping, and either we fight or flight. We just don't have time to sit down and analyze the correct reaction.

Being "scared stiff" is something that happens most often when we have to make a decision about something that we have to encounter in the future. This can either be something we think may give us pain or something that, because of past experience, we know can give us pain.

There is another saying: "Action overcomes fear." Sitting and worrying only makes the monster grow. Make a decision and take action. No matter what the outcome is, it's best to have the event behind you than in front of you.

One of the fundamental facts of life is if we don't start, we don't stand a chance of getting there. Sounds simple. Seems obvious. But still, it's a major factor in why we don't do what we know we should do. Some people call it "the paralysis of analysis." It's easy to sit in the comfort of our status quo and rationalize about what we could or should do if we had more information or if circumstances were just different. Successful people take action. If Sister Teresa hadn't picked up that first orphaned child, she would have never picked up the thousands that followed.

> "If don't we start, we don't stand a chance of getting there."

Wayne Dyer has said, "You'll seldom experience regret for anything that you've done. It's what you haven't done that will torment you. The message, therefore, is clear. Do it! Develop an appreciation for the present moment. Seize every second of your life and savor it. Value your present moments. Using them up in any self-defeating way means you've lost them forever."

> **"Most people die with much of their music still inside them."**

"Most people die with much of their music still inside them."

We must always remember that it's impossible to fail completely, and it's impossible to succeed perfectly.

And when we fail, we've been successful in making a decision. We've successfully had the courage to try something different. We've been successful in making a commitment to something.

It's better to try something and fail than to attempt nothing and succeed.

4. Giving Up too Soon

In his book *Think and Grow Rich,* the author Napoleon Hill tells the story of a man who bought a piece of property because he felt it had gold on it. After an initial investigation, he did discover a large vein of gold.

He took all his money and bought the necessary machinery to mine the gold. Unfortunately, in a short period of time, the vein disappeared. He worked and worked but couldn't find any gold.

Disillusioned, he sold the property and equipment to a junk dealer for pennies on the dollar. Out of curiosity, the junk dealer consulted a gold mining expert. The expert said the previous owner failed because he didn't understand fault lines. The gold vein should reappear a few feet beyond where he had stopped.

The new owner followed the expert's suggestion and found millions of dollars of gold just beyond where the previous owner had quit.

I'm sure it would make us crazy if we actually knew how many times during our life just how close we came to success only to quit a few-feet short of our goal. Yes, I did mean to write "goal," not "gold." For many of us, being a success doesn't necessarily equal wealth. Success can be rescuing a failing marriage. Success can be getting a wayward child back on track.

Giving up too soon is simply the result of a lack of perseverance.

Orison Swett Marden, in his 1913 book entitled *Training For Efficiency*, put it well. "Nothing great is ever accomplished without energetic persistence, and determination to do the right thing regardless of obstacles.

> "Giving up to soon is simply the result of a lack of perseverance."

A weak, vacillating person, a half-hearted man, excites no admiration or enthusiasm. Nobody believes in him. It is the positive, energetic, dead-in-earnest man who creates confidence; and without the confidence of others, it is difficult to succeed.

"The world makes way for the determined man. Everybody believes in the man who persists, sticks, hangs on, when others let go. Tenacity of purpose gives confidence. If you stick to your purpose through thick and thin, if you have the genius of persistence, you have the first qualification of an achiever."

A story is told of a disciple who went to his guru because he wanted enlightenment. The guru happened to be washing himself at the edge of a stream. He asked his disciple to kneel down next to the stream. The guru put his hand on the back of the disciple's head and pushed it under the water. The disciple thought it was a form of baptism and didn't resist. After a while, the disciple's lungs started screaming out for oxygen. He started fighting the guru to get his head out of the water. But the guru persisted. Finally, the disciple broke loose and started gasping for air. Calmly the guru said, "When you desire enlightenment as much as you desired air, you will have it."

Now, here is persistence: Jacques LeFevrier decided he wanted to commit suicide. He left nothing to chance. He stood at the top of a tall cliff and tied a noose around his neck. He tied the other end of the rope to a large rock. He drank some poison and set fire to his clothes. He even decided to shoot himself as he jumped off the cliff.

When he jumped and shot the gun, the bullet missed him and cut through the rope above him. He plunged into the sea below. The sudden dunking extinguished the flames. The cold water made him vomit the poison. A fisherman dragged him out of the water and took him to the hospital, where he died of hypothermia.

How important is the objective you're working for? If it's really important, you won't give up.

5. Having the Wrong People Around You

We're always hearing about someone being a "self-made" person. Like the myth of the level playing field, I hate to blow people's illusion, but there is no such thing as a self-made person. We all depend on other people to aid us in our successes. It may be a faithful secretary who answers the phone, types the letters, and basically makes the office run smoothly, so we have time to become self-made.

Then there's the sales people who bring in the orders and the people in the plant who make sure the product is manufactured correctly and efficiently and shipped to the customer. There is even the lowly night custodian who makes sure this "self-made man" arrives to a clean and pleasant office when he arrives at work.

Because our goals are too important for us to attempt to reach on our own, it's important we have the right people around us.

Although talent and skill is important, even more important is having people around us who are positive.

It's essential to have people who understand our goals and support them in our inner circle. Take a look at the people around you. Do they encourage you when you share your ideas or are they discrediting them? When you're around them, do they make you feel good or do they suck all your energy and enthusiasm? The people around you should believe in you and encourage your gifts.

There are also people for whom the glass is always half empty, rather than half full. Every time you're around them, all they can do is talk about all their problems and how difficult life is. And some of these people are so good at what they do, they could be standing on a ledge, ready to jump and talk their rescuer into jumping with them.

What I'm going to say now may seen harsh, but if at all possible, you need to get rid of anyone who doesn't believe in you or isn't positive. I realize there are those circumstances when it may be impossible or impractical to rid your life of these people. For instance, your spouse or a coworker may be a negative, degrading person. I'm not suggesting you get a divorce or quit your job.

First, if this is true, I feel sorry for you. Second, there is something you can do. Often people who put other people down have gotten into the habit of doing it without any rational reasoning. They say things like "Boy, was that stupid?" or "You're an idiot" because it's easy to say, and the people to whom it's said usually either timidly accept it or get angry and say something just as stupid and irrational back.

I wonder what would happen if you would respond with something like "I'm sorry you think I'm stupid. I thought we were friends, and I can't imagine anyone wanting to be a friend with someone who is stupid." And if they're truly a friend, watch them backtrack.

Negative people are looking for sympathy. They need people to confirm how terrible their lives are. And when someone agrees with them, it's like putting a supercharger on an automobile engine. So instead of giving them a supercharger, you install a governor on their engine.

First, you show sympathy. "I'm sorry that's happening in your life." Then you point out how fortunate they are in other areas. It probably won't change their negativity, but like sharks that avoid areas where there is no food, these people will avoid you.

6. Lack of Passion

Living a life without a firm knowledge of what you want to accomplish is similar to trying to take the rapids of the Colorado River through the Grand Canyon in a raft without a rudder. It can be done, but the water on the outside of the raft (circumstances) determines the course, not the people inside.

Whether you call it life planning, dream fulfillment, or goal setting, it's essential you have an understanding of where you want to go in order to make sure you aren't swept down the river of life by the pressures of circumstance.

When the architects designed the original Disneyland in Anaheim, CA, and the contractors set up the construction schedule, they scheduled the Fantasyland Castle to be the last building built. Even though the architects and contractors showed logistical and financial advantages to the contrary, Walt Disney demanded that the Fantasyland Castle be the first building constructed. He said, "I want everyone working on the project to see that castle all day and every day, so they don't forget what it is we're trying to do here."

Sometimes, we get busy taking care of our daily problems and concerns and lose the vision we have for our life. When that happens, the decisions we make in dealing with these daily problems and concerns don't always direct us to our life's vision. It's essential that we're constantly looking at our castle to make sure even the smallest decision goes along with "what we're trying to do here."

For some people, goal setting has a bad taste. They, or someone close to them, have gone to a seminar dealing with goal setting where the leader talked about how they could become a millionaire or the president of their company. He instructed the attendees to write down those things the attendees would like to have—a million dollars, Rolls Royce, or boat. Simply things.

I can distinctly recall that day, several years ago, when I filled my goal to have a Cadillac automobile. On my way home from the dealership, I remember having a feeling of emptiness. Driving my Cadillac just didn't give me the joy I had imagined. It was just a thing.

Since then, I've come to understand that simply having things as goals often result in a person abandoning the goals because the "thing" wasn't really something they wanted. It was something the goal setter thought they should want because of society, parents, or other loved ones. And usually, when the person achieved the goal, there was a let down. Goal setters refer to this phoneme as the journey being more exciting than the destination.

If, on the other hand, a person bases their goals, dreams, and plans on their principles or their core values, they look at tangible things as merely elements, making it possible to stay true to their core values.

> "Once you understand your true values, dreams are easier to fulfill."

Once you understand your true values, dreams are easier to fulfill. And we all have unfulfilled dreams.

A young minister and his daughter arrived early at his small country church to open it before Sunday services. The custom of the church was to have an offering plate at the door so attendees could place their contributions as they left the service.

In order to "prime the pump," the young minister put a dollar bill in the offering plate when he placed it on the table next to the door.

As the minister and his daughter were leaving the church following the service, the minister picked up the offering plate. All that was in it was the dollar bill the minister had placed there earlier that morning.

Noticing the lone dollar, his daughter said, "Daddy, if you would have put more in the plate, you would have gotten more out of it."

Thus, a law of life. The more we put into something, the more we get out of it.

Richard Paul Evans is the author of *The Christmas Box*, a book with the distinguished honor of being simultaneously the number-one hardcover and paperback book in the nation.

His trip in getting there had so many obstacles; his success in spite of the obstacles became the main story behind the book.

He was turned down by every publisher he took it to. When he finally decided to self-publish the book, he was turned down by the distributors. After getting into the national market, he was turned down for interviews by all the TV people. According to Richard, "It was like everything went wrong over and over and over."

But Richard Evans had two things going for him: a good book and a passion for the book. He said, "I was willing to do uncomfortable things. I was willing to take chances. I was willing to risk everything for this book."

I can guarantee if you're ambivalent about accomplishing something, when obstacles arise, and they will arise, you'll turn around and go home. If you're passionate, as Richard Evans says, you'll be willing to risk everything, and you'll succeed.

Martin Luther King said, "If a man is called to be a street sweeper, he should sweep streets even as Michelangelo painted or Beethoven composed music or Shakespeare wrote poetry. He should sweep streets so well that all the hosts of heaven and earth will pause to say, 'Here lived a great street sweeper who did his job well."

If what you do is legal and ethical, it should be done with passion and integrity, or you should find something else to do where you can do your best.

Failure Isn't Final

Dr. Denis Waitley is a productivity consultant, who has sold over ten million copies of his audio programs in fourteen different languages, and the author of fourteen best selling books.

Dr. Waitley says, "I've always looked at failure as a learning experience or target correction. I've got so much failure in my life that if failure were fertilizer, I'd have big bags of horse manure all over my room. However, failure is the fertilizer of success because it enables you to mulch it, lay it down, and grow future ideas without making the same mistakes. Look at a mistake as something you're not going to repeat."

> "Look at a mistake as something you've not going to repeat."

Winston Churchill said, "Success is the ability to go from failure to failure without losing your enthusiasm."

William Shakespeare wrote, "There is a tide in the affairs of men, which, taken at the flood, leads on to fortune; Omitted, all the voyage of their life is bound in shallows and in miseries."

Yes, it's important to take this "tide" about which William Shakespeare wrote. But if you happen to miss that great opportunity that came your way, all is not lost. As with the ocean, throughout our lives, there are tides capable of carrying us to our destination. Our desire should be to take one of the opportunities that come our way. We may not get there as easily or as soon as "our one great opportunity." But it will sure beat being "bound in shallows and in miseries."

Always remember; if you aren't dead, there's always hope.

> "If you aren't dead, there's always hope."

In Conclusion

As I write this, I have a ten-year-old grandson who participates in the youth sports. He isn't a star but a roll player. He comes by this naturally. Both his father and I were roll players as a youth. Our athletic abilities came out in high school and college.

Kaine is presently playing Little League Baseball. At a recent practice, he was hit in the temple by a baseball. Obviously it hurt. And tears were produced.

After practice, he told his dad that he wanted to quit baseball. After a long discussion, he decided to continue until the end of the season.

He approached the next game a bit timidly. Playing right field, early in the game, a fly ball was hit in his direction. Moving to his left, he raised his glove over his head and caught the ball.

He walked the first time at bat. The second time, the coach wanted to advance the runners on base, so he asked Kaine to bunt. He laid down a perfect bunt, advancing the runners and getting on base.

Later in the game, the left fielder was hurt and couldn't continue. With the team short on players, the coach had to resort to only two outfielders. Moved to center field, Kaine was responsible for center and left field.

A fly ball was hit to left-center. Running to his right, Kaine was able to reach out and barely catch the ball.

I would like to be able to say this was the last out in the last inning, and his team won the game, but it wasn't, and they ended up losing.

However, because of his performance, the coach gave him the game ball.

The point of the story is not to brag on my grandson, although that's just what I've done. But the point of the story is that if he had quit, Kaine would not have gotten the game ball.

I wonder how many "game balls" each of us has missed out on because we quit. I know for me, there are probably several.

As we come up against obstacles in the future, we should always remember to "go the distance."

Chapter 8

Be Fair in All Your Dealings

Should I ever have a retail store, I've always thought it would be fun and interesting to have the following statement on a sign just below the name of the store: "WE CHEAT THE OTHER GUY AND PASS THE SAVINGS ON TO YOU." First, I'm sure most people would laugh and think it was funny, knowing I wouldn't really be doing that. At least, if I was doing that, I wouldn't be announcing it to the world.

On the other hand, I'm sure there would be a small percentage of people who would think it would be fair. They would think they should be getting advantages at the expense of others and that I was only being fair.

Just What Is Being Fair?

As a parent or just an adult who is around children, young people, or as I think more about it, even adults, it isn't unusual to hear someone say, "But that's not fair!" What they're really saying is "What's happening to me isn't what I want to happen."

Maybe someone is giving away free candy, and we show up after the last piece was given out. Or we're standing in line for a special performance of our favorite musical group, and as we get up to the ticket window the ticket person says, "I'm sorry. The person in front of you just bought the last tickets. The performance is sold out." We stammer, "But I've been in line for two hours. This isn't fair."

I refer you back to Chapter 7—Go the Distance, where I talk about life not being fair. Again I say, "Life isn't fair." Understand there are those things in life that just happen; neither you nor other people control it.

Does Being Treated Fairly Mean Being Treated Equally?

I may surprise you here. Equal treatment isn't necessarily fair treatment.

Recently, I read an Internet blog where a young person was trying to make the case that all people should get equal pay for their work. She said a person who collects aluminum cans should get paid the same as a doctor. After all, they both work just as hard. And besides the person collecting aluminum cans is helping the environment.

Another blogger responded to her by saying, "It takes a few minutes to train someone to collect and smash cans. To be a doctor takes at least eighteen years of schooling. Although he may not like it, a doctor can collect cans. But would you want a can collector to do brain surgery on you?"

No parent would say to a five-year-old child, "You can go out tonight, but you must be back home by ten o'clock." However, they would say that to their sixteen year-old. Are they being fair? Of course, they are.

Two patients have headaches. They visit their doctor. After an examination, the doctor discovers one has a brain tumor and the other a migraine headache. Does he treat them the same? I hope not. The first needs to be rushed to the hospital, and the second he prescribes some medicine.

Carrying the "being treated equally" logic to its end, there wouldn't be male and female athletic teams. It would be simply the best of the best. I would sure miss seeing women's professional tennis, golf, and basketball competitions.

I think we can all agree treating people fairly doesn't mean we have to treat them all equally.

My purpose here is not to address racial or other types of discrimination. My feeling is that anyone who would practice that isn't smart. They're not only putting limitations on the person being discriminated against, they're also putting limitations on themselves by not availing themselves of the possibilities the other person can offer them.

Let's Legislate Fairness

Legislating fairness? Good idea? It's been tried with limited success. No matter how many laws Congress makes, if people want to, they can find ways to get around them.

Actually, many times the laws themselves legislate unfairness. Brian Barry, in his essay "Equal Treatment and Same Treatment," says, "The notion that people are treated equally if they all have the same rights looks attractive, but it is not sufficient in itself." He points out the following examples:

1. A law mandating all animals killed for meat have to be stunned first. This is inconsistent with kosher and halal requirements for orthodox Jews and Muslims, which demand that the animal be conscious when killed.
2. A law requiring motorcyclists to wear helmets is incompatible with turbaned Sikhs riding motorcycles.
3. Some Amish in Minnesota claim the requirement of putting reflective triangles on the back of their buggies (in line with the law on slow-moving vehicles) violated their religious beliefs by being too bright and substituting faith in man with faith in God.

Since, contrary to popular belief, we don't seem to be able to legislate fairness, it seems like it's up to us to be fair on our own. So let's take a look at what it would be like to be fair in our business and personal lives.

"A man's got to have a code, a creed to live by, no matter the job."

—John Wayne

Fairness in Business

As if you don't already know this, the business world is tough. It's tough as a worker. Especially today, finding a job, keeping that job, making your boss happy and getting a sense of accomplishment is (excuse the pun) a full-time job.

And it sure isn't easy for business owners and management either, as they fight to keep business coming in and making a profit.

In this whole process, it's easy to be less than fair, I know. I've been on both sides of the desk. So let's look at what it means to be fair both as an employee and an employer.

Being Fair As an Employee

Because at the time of deciding to write this book, I made a commitment to be honest in my thoughts and comments, this is the moment of truth. Virtually all my employers I had prior to my fiftieth birthday weren't given a fair break; and for two of those companies, I was the founder and owner.

It wasn't that I was a slacker or lazy. It was because the jobs I took, including the two companies I started, was because I had a family to provide for, and these were the best opportunities I could find to do that.

I can guarantee I'm not the only person who has found himself in that situation. As a matter of fact, I wouldn't be surprised if the majority of people today are working at jobs they don't like.

So the first step in being fair in business as an employee is to have a job that you love. Easy for me to say, right? I can hear someone saying, "I have a family, a house, and car payments. And with unemployment what it is, I'm lucky just to have a job."

I'm not asking anyone to quit their job. And by the time you get to the end of this section, you'll not only have some ideas on how to end up with a job you love, you'll get some guidelines on how to be honest in your present business dealings.

My belief is everyone is on this planet for a purpose. That purpose could be something as large as the president of a multibillion-dollar corporation or as humble as the exemplary parent of one or more children. And obviously an exemplary parent is greater than a corrupt corporate president. Yes, someone can fulfill their purpose in fact but not in spirit.

Psychologist Abraham Maslow, who came up with the hierarchy of needs, also theorized that destructive behavior is the symptom of a soul-deep dissatisfaction resulting from a person not meeting their higher calling.

There is a difference between an occupation and a vocation. An occupation is a job—what we do to make money to support our life style. A vocation is a higher calling. It's what a person does to truly define who they are.

The real trick is not fulfilling your purpose but discovering it. A vast majority of people never find their purpose because they never seek to find it. You need to make sure you don't get so wrapped up in surviving and not to seeking your purpose; you end up living your life in quiet desperation.

A bird would not have the instinct to fly south in the winter unless there was a south to fly to. Nor would we have been given the yearning and desire for a meaningful and satisfying life without the ability to attain it.

Finding a Life of Purpose

So how do you find your purpose in life? There are whole books written about this process. Obviously, we don't have that much room here. However, that doesn't preclude us from taking a look at a process that might just get you started on that road.

I say "started on that road." There are those who believe life has no meaning. For those of you who believe this, I can only feel sorry. But even if you have this belief, you will benefit in going through this exercise. It may take you a bit longer than the person who's earnestly seeking his purpose. With persistence; you may be surprised at the outcome.

So what is the process? Go to a place where you're alone, turn off your cell phone, and make sure you have no appointments for the next couple of hours.

Now, sit down with a pad of paper and pen you know works. At the top of the paper write "What is my purpose in life?" Then start writing down thoughts as they come into your head. Don't pass any judgment on what you write down. It doesn't have to be a complete or grammatically correct sentence. A phrase will work just fine. Keep doing this until you run completely out of ideas or you write something down that causes you to hesitate and get a little excited. Chances are if the statement that got you excited isn't your purpose, at least it's in the ball park.

A couple of days later, go through the process again with "What is my purpose in life?" at the top of the page and the phrase that stirred you before just below. Then, thinking about that magic phrase, start brainstorming again.

So let's assume you discovered your purpose; however, what you're doing is as far from that purpose as east is from west. So what do you do? First, unless you have a major endowment, do not, I repeat, do not quit your present job.

Assuming you don't have a master's degree in the area of your passion, it isn't as impossible to become an expert in that area as you may think. I understand this won't work in every case, but on the other hand, it sure won't hurt.

If you would take just thirty minutes each day to read books and articles and search the Internet on the subject about which you need to become knowledgeable, in just one year, you would have spent over 180 hours educating yourself on your passion. Within a short period of time, you would have the equivalent of a doctor's degree. And if you would read aloud ten of those thirty minutes, you would also improve dramatically your speaking voice.

Don't you have thirty minutes to spare? You might have to give up your favorite reality show on TV. However, you may just find as you make your life more enjoyable you'll need to escape your own reality less often.

What to Do Until You Get on Purpose?

Whether you're on purpose or are working at your present occupation because it puts food on the table and pays your bills most of the time, you need to be fair with your employer.

At least eight hours a day, five days a week are spent at work. That's a significant amount of your life. And whether you love your job or endure it, you need to treat your job with pride and provide the company giving you a paycheck with the best you have to offer. That way, when you go home at the end of the day, you'll be proud of what you accomplished during that day. And you'll be amazed about how less likely you'll come home, yell at your spouse and kids, and kick the dog.

I had a neighbor who had less than five years before he would be vested in his job for retirement. Unfortunately, he hated what he did. Ron had thirty plus years invested in his marriage. He had two children, who were doing well on their own. His job paid well enough so his wife had never had to get a job outside the home. Each day, he would come home and complain to his wife about how much he hated his job and how unhappy he was.

As his next-door-neighbor, I could avoid him, and I did. But his wife couldn't. Slowly his wife became as bitter as he was. And before he could get that precious vestment in his retirement, his wife left him, and they got a divorce. What a price he paid for the dislike of his job!

It Could Be the Way You Look At Your Job

For several years, the owner of a small drug store hated his work. He spent his time looking for other opportunities. One day, he asked himself, "Why am I trying to get into another business when this is the business I know best?"

Once he made the decision to take advantage of the opportunity he had at hand, he started learning all he could about the drug store business. When he changed his attitude toward his business, he became successful.

The man was Charles R. Walgreen, the founder of America's largest drug store chain. He based his success more on his attitude toward his work than the work itself.

> "He based his success more on his attitude toward his work than the work itself."

There is no such thing as a "dead-end job." There are only people who create a dead end to their job. You may be flipping hamburgers for a minimum wage. If you do the job to the best of your ability and prepare yourself to go beyond that job, opportunities beyond your wildest imagination will come your way.

Looking back years later, Charles Walgreen said, "It was easy. It was fun."

He learned a basic truth. Opportunity lies right at your own door; you'll just look at what you're doing as an interesting game and play it with all your might.

Be a Contractor

Whether you're a night custodian, secretary, assembly line worker, foreman, or plant superintendent, here's an idea that will change your whole thought about your job. It's an idea I wish I was aware of when I wasn't giving my employers 100 percent. That idea is to treat your job as if you were an independent contractor with an order to fill.

With this attitude, you will look at your supervisor, not as a boss, but as your customer. And because you've been a customer all your life, you know how customers like to be treated.

So what do you do? First, you need to look at what you do each day as a business, not school recess. By this, I don't mean during work hours, you have to be somber and keep your nose to the grindstone. Everyone needs to enjoy their job. But we all know people, hopefully not us, who, during work hours, make personal phone calls, check their e-mails, leave for break early and return late, and do a myriad of other things that are like a school kid thumbing his nose at the principal.

In your life away from work, as a customer, when you found a retail clerk who didn't know what he's talking about, you probably turned in disgust and left the store.

To be a good contractor and be able to fulfill your order adequately, you need to know your job and do it well. And if you do that, you'll find your customer, your boss, will reward you handsomely.

Remember, just because you have the skills to do your job today doesn't mean you'll have the required skills in a year from now.

Even with the tight job market we're presently experiencing, there are thousands of assembly line jobs going unfilled because the manufacturer can't find people with the appropriate computer and other technical skills.

"There's no future in living in the past."

Take advantage of any opportunity to learn new skills, even if they don't directly apply to what you're presently doing. Someone who knows several skills is more important than someone who knows only one.

I've spoken to a number of people who are in corporate management about why they would let someone go who has worked for them for twenty or more years. I usually ask them a question something like this: "Why would you let someone go who has performed twenty years of obviously satisfactory work?" More often than not, their response was something like this: "Twenty years ago, he had the skills to do the job and was enthusiastic about what he was doing. Over the years, with the development of technology, he didn't take the opportunities to improve his knowledge and skills. And as he got behind in his skills, he lost the enthusiasm for what he was doing. I'm sorry, but when an employee is costing me money, and I have people wanting a job who have the current skills, I have to make an unpopular decision."

Cash Their Check, Support Their Policy

If I worked for a company that consistently had unethical and illegal policies, I'm afraid I would have to quit. It may sound drastic, but working for a company that is unethical in its policies and engages in illegal practices reflects on you and your standards.

Even if your position with the company doesn't require you to practice those policies, your involvement, at any level, although maybe not legally culpable, helps make the practice of those policies possible.

In addition, we've all been in situations where we acquire some new friends, who we think do strange things. The longer we're with the friends, the less their actions seem strange. And eventually, we even start doing the same. That can happen with your job. By being around and tacitly approving of unethical activities, eventually, you'll be able to rationalize them until they don't seem that unethical.

One of the Old West's more famous con men was Soapy Smith. The reason they call him Soapy was a particular con for which he was famous. He would take bars of soap, cut them in smaller pieces, wrap them in paper, and in a piece or two, would place $5 or $10. He would then get together a crowd and sell the soap. Of course, his associates would be the ones who got the money.

Soapy didn't feel what he was doing was wrong. He had rationalized his activities by stating that he had never coned an honest person. It was only the greedy and unethical people who fell for his cons. Watch that you don't develop the "Soapy Smith" attitude.

"Hmmm...let's see. According to the listing, this is either the outdoor hot tub or the year-round pond."

I will have to say that fortunately, I've never been in the position where I've found myself working for an unethical company. However, I believe I've disagreed with some of the policies of every company I've worked for. These weren't unethical or illegal policies, but it had more to do with procedure. And on numerous occasions, I've talked to the appropriate people about the policy. However, that talk took place in a private meeting. And if I wasn't able to convince them of my point of view, when I left the meeting, I supported the final decision. If I couldn't, I would have stopped cashing my paycheck.

In my mind, an employee who is working for a company indicates they support the company's policies.

Incidentally, if you are aware of the company you're working for is engaged in illegal practices, it would be unethical on your part not to let the proper authorities know about the illegal practices. It could save lives, and it will surely save people from misery.

But the vast majority of us are working for companies that are ethical and legal, but they're not perfect. In those cases, quit whining about what's wrong with work and start talking about what's right. And when you do talk to your supervisor about a problem, make sure you have a suggestion for a solution. That makes you a problem solver, not a complainer.

> "Honesty is not something you should flirt with—you should be married to it."

Being Fair As a Business

Throughout life, there is a struggle between good and evil. Evil is powerful. Evil is actually more powerful than good. That's because evil has no standards. Evil can lie, cheat, steal, and create any level of havoc necessary to be satisfied. Good, on the other side, has standards and ethics it must observe. Good must obey the rules. It's usually easier to allow evil to happen than to do good.

The surprise is not that there is evil in the world. The surprise is that there is so much good. That's because the basic nature of mankind is goodness. Yet in spite of that goodness, there are mass murders, child molesters, and people who do even more monstrous things. Again, thankfully, these people are the exception rather than the rule.

As we know, all businesses are comprised of people. Therefore, just as there's bad people there will be bad companies.

I don't have the skills or the power to change a bad company into a good company. However, because good companies are run by good people, I believe that quite possibly, I can make some suggestions on how to make a good company into a great company.

Next to a Company's Product, Their Employees Are Their Greatest Asset

Generally speaking, there are two different kinds of employees. There are those who work for personal fulfillment and even love what they do, as in "I love my job." There are also those who clock in at 8:00 and out at 5:00. And in between, they do what they have to do to keep their job.

Obviously, an employer would much rather have someone working for them who is dedicated than someone who endures.

First off, we all need to understand virtually everyone works for money. Everyone has bills to pay, food to buy, and loved ones to support. So no matter how good the working conditions are, unless an employer can provide a fair living wage, he will never be able to consistently employ quality people.

However, as important as money is, people want more from a job than money. They want to work for a company that treats them fairly. Fairness is a value in and of itself. And people respond positively if they feel they've been treated fairly.

As we've addressed earlier, treating people equally doesn't necessarily mean they feel they've been treated fairly.

When I owned a construction-related company, I had a young mother come to me and say that she needed a job, but because she had children of school age, she couldn't work from 8:00 to 5:00. She was highly qualified, and I needed someone with her skills. So the fair thing for both of us was to make it possible for her to come to work at 9:00 and leave at 3:00. That way, she's at home when her children leave for school and when they come home.

Everyone else, including me, came to work at 8:00 and left at 5:00. Actually, I came in before 8:00 and stayed well beyond 5:00, but that's another story.

I didn't treat Mary equally. As a result, I got a wonderful employee, and she got a job that worked within her parameters and filled in her family's economic gap.

I realize I owned a small business with the capability of being versatile in a way that a company with five thousand employees quite possibly can't. At the same time, I've found many weak and lazy large company management people hide behind "company policy." How many times have you heard someone say, "I would like to, but it's against company policy?"

"One machine can do the work of fifty ordinary men, but no machine can do the work of one extraordinary man."

What the lazy management person is really saying is "I don't care to do anything about it." We all know, with few exceptions, company policy isn't written in stone.

More often than not, exceptions to rules don't happen because the supervisor doesn't want to take the time and effort to petition the appropriate people for the exception. And when the supervisor does petition for an exception, the number-one reason for not granting it is "If we allow one person to do it, everyone will want to do it." The old "We have to treat everybody equally" thing.

And if everyone does it, one of two things will happen: 1. The whole company will fall apart. 2. Nothing will happen, and everyone will realize there was no need for the policy in the first place.

Policies do have to be established and followed to provide, if nothing else, continuity within a company. Unfortunately, when someone questions a policy, the answers range from "That's the way it's always been done" to "Are you one of those agitators?"

"If you don't have a good reason for doing something, then you have a good reason for not doing it."

In dealing with policies, communication is vitally important. Front line supervision people should be aware of the reasons for policies. If a company can't be open and honest about the reason for a policy, maybe there is no honest reason for the policy.

Employees are too often treated like mushrooms. Keep them in the dark, and feed them, uh, male cow manure. What that does is create employees who don't feel a part of the process or the company. And so the employee merely puts in his time.

What does this mean for the company? Well, first, it means an employee will put in just enough effort to get the job done. And since an employee doesn't feel a part of the process, should that employee see ways to make the company more efficient and thereby save the company money that employee won't do it. And let me tell you, it's the people who "get their hands dirty" who know what's really happening.

Practicing Win-Win

I'm the typical male. When Sunny and I have a difference of opinion, one of us has to end up being right, and by logic, the other person is wrong. She, on the other hand, asks why there has to be winners and losers.

Unfortunately, having to win and thereby making the other person a loser, is the way of life for many people.

In spite of how Sunny feels, I believe people can be right or wrong, but I don't feel there has to be winners and losers. In all dealings, particularly business dealings, I prefer being in win-win situations.

When someone plays hardball in either a business or even a personal arrangement, it usually puts the other person or people at a distinct disadvantage. A disadvantage that more often than not comes back to bite the hardball player in the, uh, posterior. This is because all trust is gone out of the relationship.

Think back, any time you've ended up on the short end of the stick, how enthusiastic were you about fulfilling the agreement? I'm sure because you're a person of principle; you would follow through with your part of the agreement. However, there are many people who wouldn't.

"In everything good or bad, there's a lesson in it."

Someone who works for win-win sees business and personal dealings as a cooperative, not competitive, arrangement.

Win-win people are always looking for benefits for everyone. Is that because they're such nice people? Well, yes and no. They may be nice people, but even more important, they're smart people. In a win-win arrangement, everyone involved will feel positive about the outcome.

According to Stephen Covey, a person or an organization who approaches agreements with a win-win attitude has three character traits:

A. Integrity: Sticking with high values and commitments.
B. Maturity: Always being considerate of other's feelings when expressing your ideas and feelings.
C. Abundant mentality: Believing there's enough for everyone.

Quite often, people live their life as if in every interpersonal dealing, the choice is to be either nice or tough. In reality, win-win requires that you be both nice and tough. You have to be nice by making sure the other person isn't taken advantage of and tough enough to make sure you aren't taken advantage of. As Steven Covey states it, one must be considerate, sensitive, and brave.

People Help Those Who Help Them

I have a number of friends who are very successful in what they do. Recently, while talking to one of these friends, the person was complaining about all the people who come to him seeking advice and how many times the answer to what their seeking can be found very easily on the Internet or by a visit to a library. He said if he had the time, he would like to help them. But if he had the time, he would be spending it doing something that would be productive for him.

As a result, he ignores about 95 percent of these requests. What about the other 5 percent? They're requests where the other person not only wants something, but they're willing to do something for him in return.

That great sales trainer Zig Ziglar has said, "You will get everything in life that you want if you just help enough other people get what they want."

Chapter 9

Be a Good Friend and Neighbor

During the three hundred years the United States had a frontier, even though the pioneers were the strong, independent type, they realized they needed the help of their neighbors, and their neighbors needed them. With neighbors miles away, people still got together for cabin raising, barn raising, log rolling, clearing fields, corn husking, and quilting bees.

Today, we have fences in common with neighbors whom we barely know. We want to believe this is because we work and commute such long hours. I can assure you the frontier people worked longer hours, and a five-mile commute in wagon or on horseback to the closest neighbor was more difficult than walking next door.

"Most folks are like a barbed wire fence. They have pretty good points."

One of the big reasons for neighbor not knowing neighbor is we no longer need our neighbor to survive. We hire someone to build our house and maintain our yard. We go to the grocery store and buy food semi or fully prepared.

We may not need the labors of neighbors, but there is a greater, even more important need for good neighbors and friends.

Recent surveys show a large percentage of people are what the surveyors classify as "significantly lonely." And they say that number is growing. Research shows having quality relationships greatly increases our likelihood of living a happy life. Because of a lack of being a friend and having friends, we are, as David Thoreau put it, living lives of quiet desperation.

Even though the frontier life was difficult, the pioneer was confident in the future. They believed it was limitless. Hospitality and generosity was a natural outcrop of that confidence. Today, we're living in financially difficult and politically divisive times. During these times, we need more than ever to be a good friend and neighbor. Quite possibly, our friends will be a major influence in keeping us sane.

According to the dictionary, a *friend* is a person who one knows, likes, and trusts. A *neighbor* is one who is located near to another; a fellow human being.

Let's start with taking a look at being a friend.

Just What Does It Mean to Be a Good Friend?

Quite often, the word *friend* is used in such a casual manner that it has lost much of its significance. We meet someone who is attractive and has a good personality, and within a half hour, they've become our "new best friend." Some people collect friends like they're marbles or rocks. If we have a lot of friends, it shows just how popular we are. Besides, they could be useful, should we need something.

In reality, there are "friends," and then there are "acquaintances." I recently saw the Tom Selleck movie *Monte Walsh* for about the fifteenth time. In the movie, the ranch manager played by William Devane says the cowboys on his ranch have no money and no possessions except their saddle, but they were willing to put their lives on the line for each other. And back in the 1870s and 1880s,

"Everyone has two kinds of friends: those who are around when you need them and those who are around when they need you."

that's the way it was for many a working cowboy. As we shall see later, this is an element of a friend.

Friends bring out the best in friends. A great coach has the ability to make a player think he is better than he is. He lets his players know that he believes in them, and before long, they discover talent they never knew they had.

A vast majority of people who end up in prison say when they were young, people predicted they would end up in prison. One wonders what would have happened if people had told them they had the ability to become someone of greatness.

I have heard it said if during a person's lifetime, they have but one truly good friend—Someone they can trust implicitly and confide in without reservation—that person is truly lucky.

I am the first to admit, I'm not the most trusting person. However, I'm very fortunate to be able to say over the last thirty plus years; I have had such a friend. And I'm doubly fortunate to be able to say that friend is my wife, Sunny.

A true friend is someone who accepts us just as we are with all our faults and problems and loves us in spite of our character defects. They like us because of our good characteristics and love us in spite of our bad characteristics.

It's essential before we have friends; we have to be a friend. So let's take a look at the elements of being a good friend:

1. The Golden Rule

Just in case, you've been raised under a bushel basket, the Golden Rule is "Do unto others as you would have them do unto you." It should be the basis of all our dealings with fellow human beings.

Robert Conklin, in his book *How to Get People to Do Things*, says the one great principle in dealing with others is "To the degree you give others what they want, they will give you what you want." All our lives we've heard axioms like the Golden Rule, such as "It's in giving that we receive."

Still we say, "I would be glad to show my spouse more affection, if she/he would only give me some first."

"I would trust him, but he must show he deserves my trust."

"I would encourage my kids if they would just show me a little respect."

The law is we must first give to others what they want, and then we'll get what we want. Give love to our spouse, and we'll get it back. Trust, and we'll find others respect our trust. Encourage our kids, and they'll respond like a plant does to sunlight and water. But getting in return shouldn't be the only motive.

Mother Theresa had a different philosophy. On the wall of her children's home in Calcutta was the following saying:

"People are unreasonable, illogical, and self-centered—Love them anyway.

If you do good, people will accuse you of selfish, ulterior motives—Do good anyway.

If you are successful, you win false friends and true enemies—Succeed anyway.

The good you do will be forgotten tomorrow—Do good anyway.

Honesty and frankness make you vulnerable—Be honest and frank anyway.

What you spend years building may be destroyed overnight—Build anyway.

People really need help but may attack you if you help them—Give the world the best you've got anyway."

The majority of people in the world are waiting for someone else to take the first step. The bottom line is if you want to have good friends, first you must be a good friend.

John Fleming was a poor Scottish farmer. While working in the fields, he heard the cry of a young boy who was stuck in the nearby bog.

Farmer Fleming, at the risk of his own life, saved the young boy from the bog. The boy thanked him and left for home.

The next day, a fancy carriage pulled up in front of the farmer's home. A nobleman climbed out of the carriage and introduced himself as the father of the young man whose life Fleming had saved the day before.

"I would like to pay you for saving my son's life," said the nobleman.

"I cannot accept payment. My hopes are that someone would do the same for my son should he need it."

"I'll make you a deal. Let me provide your son with the same education my son would receive. It will be doing for your son as you did for mine."

Farmer Fleming agreed, and his son ended up graduating from St. Mary's Hospital Medical School in London. Eventually, he became Sir Alexander Fleming, the discoverer of Penicillin.

Years later, the nobleman's son, who was stuck in the bog, came down with pneumonia. It was Penicillin that saved the nobleman's son.

What was the nobleman's name? Lord Randolph Churchill. And what was his son's name? Winston Churchill.

I'm reminded of a little saying in the Old Testament book of Ecclesiastes. "Cast your bread upon the waters, for after many days you will find it again."

But how do you know if you're a good friend. You can easily tell. If people enjoy being around you, and if when they're in your presence, they're cheerful and filled with enthusiasm, chances are you are portraying the correct characteristics.

Before you say or do something, ask yourself if you would want the other person to say or do that to you. At first, it might seem awkward, and there might be a pause in your actions, but after a while, thinking in this way will become natural.

Incidentally, this concept is so important it should not only be practiced in your personal relationships but with acquaintances as well. And you never know these acquaintances may just become good friends.

Dale Carnegie said, "You have it easily in your power to increase the sum total of this world's happiness now. How? By giving a few words of sincere appreciation to someone who is lonely or discouraged. Perhaps you will forget tomorrow the kind words you say today, but the recipient may cherish them over a lifetime."

Very few people have the ability to persist without encouragement.

Even though he's been retired from professional basketball for a number of years, I still marvel at the amazing things Michael Jordan could do on a basketball court. There is no doubt, Michael was born with a talent.

It's interesting to know that the majority of extraordinary performers in any area weren't born with an exceptional talent. Dr. Benjamin Bloom of the University of Chicago studied one hundred outstanding young athletes, musicians, and students—people who were considered prodigies. He found most of them didn't begin with flashes of great brilliance.

"...whether it's friendship or material items, if we give in order to receive, we may just get a pumpkin in return."

Everyone is born with unlimited potential. Parents, grandparents, uncles, aunts, and friends can help develop or destroy that potential. That's an awesome responsibility.

Each time we come into contact with someone, we shouldn't leave their company without giving them a word of encouragement.

Even Michael Jordan needed encouragement. He couldn't make his high school varsity basketball team his sophomore year. Were it not for the support of his father, he might not have continued playing basketball. And just think what we basketball fans would have missed.

You will always have what you want if you help others have what they want.

2. Don't Give Just to Receive

Sadly, there are people who are friends with someone just for what they can get from that person. They go into relationships, asking themselves, "How can my being a friend with John make me more popular or help me make those important business connections?"

During ancient times, a king was having his fiftieth birthday. He requested that each family within the kingdom bring him a present.

There were two brothers who lived within his kingdom. One was very wealthy. The other was a poor farmer, who grew pumpkins.

The poor farmer, wanting to show his appreciation of the king and not knowing what else to give him, brought the best he had, the biggest pumpkin in his patch.

The king, knowing the sacrifice of the farmer, said, "This is the best gift I have ever received. Because of this, I will give you one-fourth of my kingdom."

The rich brother, seeing the reward his poor brother received for a mere pumpkin and hoping to receive an even larger portion of the kingdom, filled a wheelbarrow with gems and gold, virtually depleting his wealth.

Showing excitement with the gift, the king said, "This is such a great gift I must reward you with the greatest gift I have ever received." And he gave the man the pumpkin.

Always remember, whether it's friendship or material items, if we give in order to receive, we may just get a pumpkin in return.

3. Be Yourself

When I started thinking about this point, I named it "Be Authentic." Me being a simple country boy, the word *authentic* just seemed to be a bit nebulous and fancy. When I told my wife, Sunny, she said, "Don't use fancy words. Just be yourself." And so the title.

During this section, I'm going to be quoting different people who use the word *authentic*. For consistency, I'll be changing the word to *yourself*. You'll know when this happens because I'll italicize the word *yourself*.

Being ornery, mean and nasty isn't the problem for most of us. Our problem is the opposite. More often, we find ourselves compromising our principles in order to be liked by people.

We may get away with it at a party or casual social situation, but people pick up on it as we start paring down to a one-on-one relationship. The reason people can pick up on insincerity is that we've all been there.

We can leave a social situation, but a business situation can be different. Unless we're willing to quit our job, and few of us are in a position to do that, we will have to "suck it up" around a boss, coworker, or customer, who isn't willing to accept us as we really are. But at the same time, this is no reason we can't show the characteristics of a friend.

Before we get very far in this area, it would be good to discover just why it is we find it so difficult to be ourselves.

A part of our not being ourselves is that as we were growing up, we were learning what is acceptable and not acceptable in society, when we did something unacceptable, we were told we were bad. I know. My parents did me this way, and I did it with my sons.

I'm not saying we shouldn't correct our children. It's what we say when we correct them. Instead of saying they were bad, parents should say, "What you did was bad." And proceed from there. It may be a subtle difference but an important one.

Unfortunately, parents get frustrated or embarrassed and do and say things that are over the top.

Recently, Sunny and I went to a children's horseshow called a gymkhana. And when I say children, they started at six years of age.

The six year-olds had a parent walking beside them, holding them and the horse, while going through the course. As one six-year-old, on her horse, was walked up to the first obstacle, she started crying, saying she didn't want to do this. Immediately, the mother became embarrassed. The mother yelled at her daughter to stop crying. When that didn't work, she grabbed her daughter off the horse, and while hastily walking out of the arena, the mother said, "We're going home, and you're going to spend the afternoon pulling weeds."

That day, the daughter got a lesson not to be herself.

Don't misunderstand me; I'm not suggesting we blame our parents. As I've said earlier, when we blame anyone for who we are, we give them all the power. It's just that when something goes wrong, it's very beneficial to know how it went wrong.

One of the reasons an honest relationship is so difficult is that many people are portraying an image of themselves and are afraid of showing the real person that they are—a person who at times says and does stupid things. Being the ideal person is an impossibility. What is possible is living our life as we really are. Surprisingly, this allows other people to be who they are around us.

What I've found—and I'm still working on convincing myself 100 percent of the time—is being true to who I really am is the key to truly happy relationships.

Being *yourself* is essential to being a good friend. We can't go through life, wearing disguises and playing roles. We need to be transparent and true to our core values. For if we're not, those people we call our friends are friends of our disguise and not us.

In addition, when we're true to our core values, we're living a life that resonates to our inner being. We don't complicate our lives with destructive relationships or lifestyles. We'll gain an inner strength by letting go of manipulation and power plays.

Always remember you can fool some of the people some of the time but not all the people all the time. And that goes for fooling yourself as well.

Victoria Reynolds has a great definition of what it means to be yourself. "Being *yourself* is the ability to be true to oneself. Living a life *true to yourself* requires the ability to be true to our own wants, needs, and desires and not live our lives by the opinion of others. Being *true to ourselves* gives us the insight and compassion to see others, for who they are, not who we expect them to be. It frees us up from the judgment of ourselves and others, and it gives others the freedom to be themselves as well."

Possibly I need to place a little reminder here that "to be true to our own wants, needs, and desires" isn't a license to be selfish. Notice she also says that being true to ourselves creates within ourselves a compassion for others.

According to Dr. Carl Hammerschlag, "*Being true to yourself* occurs when the head and the heart meet the lips; when what we think and feel is congruent with what we say."

What Dr. Hammerschlag is saying is if what we say and what we do aren't the same we have a problem, not just with other people, but with ourselves. Are we being the type of friend we would like to have as a friend? Would we want everyone to emulate the same degree of friendship we portray?

Let's go back to the person who maintains his true personality is ornery, mean, and nasty. I tend to believe anyone who portrays such a personality is much like a small dog who barks and threatens to attack a much larger dog. They're not barking because they think they're a big dog. They're barking because they're afraid, and they're hoping they're able to bluff the much bigger dog.

In the same way, someone displaying an aggressive attitude is just trying to cover up the fact they're a softy and afraid they'll be hurt emotionally.

There also has to be a balance between being frank and being sensitive and caring. Rather than saying to a friend, "That's the ugliest dress I've ever seen," you can say, "You know, you look prettier in the blue dress." Most assuredly, you will have sent the same message with much less distress.

4. Be Trustworthy and Loyal

Trustworthiness and loyalty go hand in hand. When we know someone will be loyal to us, we know we can trust them.

When I think of being trustworthy and loyal, I immediately think of a Boy Scout. In some circles saying someone is a "Boy Scout" doesn't mean he's a member of that organization, but that he portrays the precepts of that organization.

Wilson Rawls in his book about a boy and his two dogs, *Where the Red Fern Grows*, has one of his characters say, "People have been trying to understand dogs ever since the beginning of time. You can read every day where a dog saved the life of a drowning child, or lay down his life for his master. Some people call this loyalty. I don't. I may be wrong, but I call it love—the deepest kind of love.

"It's a shame that people all over the world can't have that kind of love in their hearts. There would be no wars, slaughter or murder; no greed or selfishness. It would be the kind of world that God wants us to have—a wonderful world."

I'm not saying we should be puppy dogs, eagerly waiting for someone to pet us or give us a treat. On the other hand, if we showed a similar level of excitement about our friends, we may just have more.

Unfortunately, that perfect world Wilson Rawls pined for isn't going to take place because there are too many people in the world who are greedy and selfish.

Loyalty is one of the main qualities one looks for when we're searching for friends. And there is no reason for each of us not to have a loyalty similar to that described by Mr. Rawls. And wouldn't you love to have a friend or two like that?

> "Remember, anyone who will gossip with you will not hesitate to gossip about you."

It's natural to enjoy talking about people. It gives us a feeling of superiority. By telling a story about someone, it confirms that we wouldn't do the terrible things that person did. As we share and get shared with, there is a feeling of comradely with the person to whom we're talking. Our sharing means we're close friends. And when we can add more details than anyone else, even if it's speculation, we display our importance. It also gives us an opportunity to show we're a caring person. "I'm so sorry for Sam's family. They have to endure so much because he . . ."

Those are not the only benefits that talking about people (gossiping) provides. First, it shows we have no integrity. Second, we've just discovered someone who will probably talk about us when we're not around. Third, we've exposed ourselves to the possibility the person we gossiped to will tell what we said to the person we just talked about.

If a friend tells you something in confidence, don't talk about it to anyone. Never say anything about a friend you wouldn't say to your friend's face. And even under this condition, it's best not to say anything.

In a similar manner, you shouldn't let other people talk about a friend if you don't think what is being said is true. You can say something like this: "I know him, and it just doesn't sound right. Before this goes any further, let me talk to him and get his perspective. I'll let you know what he says." Then observe the look on the other person's face.

There's another element of being trustworthy and loyal. You look out for your friends. If they have had too much to drink at a party, as the campaign slogan goes, "a friend doesn't let a friend drive drunk" even if that friend protests.

As well, if a friend tells you he's thinking about suicide or some other drastic act, all bets are off. Get your friend help.

But as a general rule, trust is the basis of a good relationship. So don't do anything that will lose a friend's trust.

There can never be trust in a relationship based upon gossip. It has been said that to be trusted is greater than to be loved. However, to be trusted is also to be loved.

A man was walking down a road with his dog when he realized he was dead. He remembered dying and that his dog had died years before. As he continued down the road, he came upon a large mother of pearl gate with a gold street leading to it.

As the traveler and his dog entered the gate, he saw a man setting at a desk. "Where are we?" asked the traveler.

"This is heaven," said the man at the desk.

"May I have some water?"

"You may, but you can't bring your dog inside," responded the gatekeeper. Not wanting to leave his companion behind, the traveler with his dog turned and continued down the road.

Later, the traveler came upon a farmhouse. As he approached it, he saw a man setting in a chair. "May we have some water?" questioned the traveler.

"You may. And there is a bowl next to the well to water your dog."

"What do you call this place?" asked the traveler.

"This is heaven."

"But the place down the street with the pearly gate is heaven," said the traveler.

"Oh, that is actually hell."

The traveler asked, "Doesn't it make you mad for them to use your name?"

"Actually not, we're just happy that they screen out the folks who'll leave their best friends behind."

Never abandon friends, even those who walk on only two legs.

5. Be a Good Listener

Do you know why we have one mouth and two ears? It's because listening is twice as hard as talking. Listening is hard. Especially when the conversation we're listening to is just plain boring or not nearly as important when compared to what we have to say.

I often find myself listening to someone impatiently, waiting for them to take a breath so I can say something really important.

We need to always keep in mind that expressing ourselves is only half of the communication process. The other half is listening and understanding. Part of being a good friend is being willing to listen rather than talk. It takes time and effort because listening isn't natural. And so often, at least in our own minds, other people don't express their wants and needs as clearly as we do. But then, we do have two ears and a superior mind.

First, we need to understand we aren't the only person who wants the attention of others. Everyone, even from the youngest baby, who cries to get attention, to the oldest person, who wants to tell everyone about his life's experiences, wants the attention of others. That's why people at ballgames wave when the camera pans the crowd.

Experts say our desire to attract attention to ourselves is our outwardly showing our desire to be important. And that's true even for those gruff old guys who maintain there is no way they want the spotlight. Just let them be ignored by a waitress at their favorite coffee shop or have a clerk at the local department store be more interested in stocking the shelves than helping them find the right-size shirt they want to buy.

So if down deep everyone wants to be the center of the universe, isn't it logical if we want to be a good friend, we need to pay attention to what our friends say?

Don't interrupt others. Particularly, don't complete their sentences. This probably happens most often with married couples. I know it happens with Sunny and me.

When someone is interrupted, in an effort not to be interrupted again, the other person will start talking just a bit faster. With the faster speech, and thinking that goes along with it, conversations begin getting an irritable edge to them. This also requires the person doing the interrupting to not only do the thinking for themselves, but the other person as well. And few, if any of us are smart enough to do that.

Always remind yourself to have patience when listening. Not interrupting a person's conversation will put the other person at ease and make their experience with you much more enjoyable.

It takes a lot of self-confidence not to want to say, "Look at me. I'm special. My story will top yours." Our ego wants us to be seen and heard. And we know as a result of our telling a great story, everyone will respect us and want to be around us. Unfortunately, that's not the way it happens. When we dive in and bring the conversation back to us, we've taken away any joy the other person has in sharing their story. As a result, a chasm develops between us and the other person.

If you're having a hard time keeping from jumping in before the other person finishes his remark, here's a little trick that just may help you in developing more patience. It's something that has helped a number of people. It's as simple as taking a breath before responding. Although that breath might initially seem like a lifetime, be assured it isn't. What it is, is being courteous.

In the beginning, it may be difficult to break the habit, but once we start surrendering the need for our ego to strut itself and experiencing the quiet confidence of allowing the other person to have a bit of glory, we'll mysteriously find more people will respect us and want to be around us.

Not only do we need to listen, we need to listen intently. To be able to listen effectively, we need to be active in the process and not just listening passively. We need not only to listen to the words; we need to listen for the message. We need to listen not only with our ears, but with our whole face and body. We need to look directly at our friend, even to the point of leaning toward them. We need to give them vocal feedback. "Yes." "Sure." "And then what happened?" "Wow." And don't forget to ask questions, seeking more information.

One of the important parts of listening is trying to understand the situation from your friend's point of view. Stephen Covey, in his book *The Seven Habits of Highly Effective People*, states one of those habits as "Seek first to understand."

This says we should be more interested in understanding the other person than making the other person understand us. This is totally counter-intuitive.

But as strange as it may seem understanding what people are trying to say and where they're coming from makes it much easier to frame your conversation as you're trying to be understood.

When we disagree with someone, we need to understand the person we're disagreeing with is every bit as certain of his point of view as we are of ours. And the more we defend each of our points of view, the more stress develops between the two of us. The next time someone expresses an opinion contrary to yours, why not seek an understanding as to why they have that position. Remember, to understand someone doesn't mean you agree with them. Incidentally, if you try to understand, you may just discover that the other person will do the same about your point of view.

It isn't about being right or wrong. It's about being effective when communicating with others. And it will translate into better friends.

It's important to paraphrase and use your own words in expressing your understanding of the conversation. If there is a misunderstanding, you or the person you're talking to will know immediately. This also helps in assisting the friend in coming up with the appropriate conclusions.

"But, but," I can hear you say, "What about me?" Well, I guess you just have to hope your friend loves you enough to give you a chance to be the center of the universe.

I close with this. Two people were talking. Actually, only one was talking. Finally, the one talking said, "But enough about me. Let's talk about you. So what do you think about me?"

6. Be Respectful

It's not unusual for friends to do a lot of joking and poking fun, especially when it's between men. Always be sensitive of what you kid about. And if you are a true friend, you know the things about which your friend is sensitive. Never, never, never kid about those things.

Always remember, things you and your friends discuss should be treated with care. Treat them as gently as if you were holding your friend's heart in your hands because some of the things they may have shared with you could very well have been because they trust you with things as sensitive as their heart.

We talked earlier about being a person of your word. Even though a person of character tries never to make a promise that he can't keep, this precept is a thousand times over with a friend. And when you find you can't keep a promise, notify your friend as soon as possible.

"I agree with what you say, but I don't think it should be done that way." How many times have you had someone say that or something similar to you? Or even worse, how many times have you said it?

Anytime you say the word *but* in a sentence similar to above, what you're doing is negating everything you said in front of the but." You're agreeing and disagreeing with your friend in the same sentence. That's characteristic of a split personality.

If you disagree with your friend, you should be able to do it in a concise manner. If, on the other hand, you used the *but* because you didn't feel your friend had expressed the full story, it's more appropriate to use *and*. By using *and*, what you're saying is, I agree with what you say, and I feel there is more to the story than you expressed.

Not only does this allow you to more concisely express your feelings, you'll find your friend will more readily accept what you have to say. Incidentally, this will work with everyone from friend to stranger.

There are also going to be times when a friend is being—well, let's not mince words—a butthead. Here's where your saintliness should show forth. Just show them the respect you want to be shown when you are one of those guys.

Also remember, as stated in the chapter about respecting yourself and others, a person can't respect other people until he respects himself.

Another element in respecting people. People who set out to accomplish things open themselves up to criticism. Reading about the lives of people from Jesus to Bill Gates shows that people not only criticized them as they were attempting their accomplishment, it normally continued after they achieved it. Critics are often people whose only accomplishment is to criticize those people who are doers. Doers don't have time to criticize. They're too busy doing.

7. Be Honest

I think I heard somewhere that "Birds of a feather flock together." In other words, if you're not an honest person, the chances are any friends you may have aren't honest either. A dishonest person has no chance of having true friends. So we need to practice honesty and truthfulness at all times.

A good friend doesn't have to share every detail of their life, but they need to always present a clear picture of who they are and what they're feeling. And if there is a problem or something doesn't seem right in the relationship, it's immediately shared.

If you believe a friend is in the process of doing something that could be a serious risk to their safety, you may need to act in a way that will cause them anger. As with children, sometimes "tough love" is necessary with a friend. You just have to tell them what you think.

Not only is the ability to be totally honest a sign of a good friendship, the ability to be totally honest with the other person, without them being offended, is also a sign of a good friendship because they know you have their best interests at heart. But even if they're offended, remember what you're doing is because you care about them and don't want them to get hurt.

8. Be Compassionate

Compassion is something that comes from the heart of a good person. Its evidence is a sense of empathy, support, and understanding. Some people may not believe it, but all of us have the seeds of compassion inside us. For some, it's just a matter of cultivation.

Always be ready to pitch in and help a friend when they're in crisis. If a friend becomes ill, be there to provide meals or take them to the hospital.

Even if it is something as simple as their dog running away. Actually, for us dog lovers, that's not simple, and you never cared for the dog, help them find the dog.

There is another element of compassion illustrated in the following story:

A Korean legend tells of a warrior who died. Before he entered heaven, the gatekeeper gave the warrior a tour of hell. There was a great table piled high with every tasty food imaginable. But the people there were starving.

"How could this be?" he asked the gatekeeper. "Are they not allowed to eat?"

The gatekeeper explained that they could eat, but they must use five-foot-long chopsticks held from the end. They can't get food to their mouths.

The warrior was then taken to heaven. There he saw a similar room with a table loaded with food. But the people were well nourished and happy. They also had to use five-foot-long chopsticks held from the end.

"The difference is," explained the gatekeeper, "in heaven, the people had learned that by feeding others, their needs could be met in a similar way."

We need also to understand that being compassionate doesn't mean we're the other person's servant or doormat.

We're all motivated by rewards. A smile, hug, words of encouragement, are positive rewards. According to Michael LeBoeuf in *Getting Results!* "You get more of the behavior you reward. You don't get what you hope for, ask for, wish for, or beg for. You get what you reward."

To emphasize his point, he relates the story of an angler who looked over the side of his boat and saw a snake swimming alongside with a frog in his mouth. The angler picked up the snake, pulled the frog out of the snake's mouth, and got ready to release the frog. Now feeling sorry for the snake, and having no food, he opened his flask of whiskey and poured a few drops down the snake's mouth. After releasing the snake, he knew the snake was happy. He also knew the frog was happy. And he was happy. A short while later, the angler heard a tapping on the side of his boat. He looked over the side and saw the snake with two frogs in his mouth.

Always remember the quality of a person is not determined by the number of friends they have but rather the number of people they are friends to.

Being a Good Neighbor

Just what is a neighbor, and how does it differ from a friend? As indicated earlier, the dictionary defines *neighbor* as "a person living near or next door to the speaker or person referred to." The Bible expands that definition to anyone we encounter. So we're going to look at both our next-door neighbors and those people we may encounter in a business parking lot. Incidentally, the precepts for being a good neighbor also apply to being a good friend and vice versa.

First, we want to look at that person next door.

1. Don't Let Little Problems Become Big Ones

When we have a difference with someone who is a good friend, we will typically either overlook the problem or talk to them about it. Unfortunately, unless a neighbor is also a good friend, we tend to fume about our problems.

I know of two neighbors who recently went to court because of a lawsuit and countersuit. This was the climax of an ongoing battle that had taken place over a two-year period.

What started it was when the neighbor's dog was playing in the backyard with an empty plastic milk carton. After an angry outburst, the other neighbor complained about the wind chimes in the initial complainer's backyard. And it escalated from there. The end result was thousands of dollars in lawyer and court costs and two neighbors whose homes are less than twenty yards from each other literally hating each other.

But that's not as bad as the parent who goes years refusing to talk to their child, or the adult child who won't speak to his siblings or parents.

First, whether friend, acquaintance, neighbor, or relative, never, never, never let little resentments or problems escalate into big ones. Some people—not you and me, of course—are so stubborn that they refuse to reach out to the other person. They say, "He offended me. He should reach out to me."

"It's smart to spend less time trying to figure out who's right and more time trying to figure out what's right."

Which is more important, being right or being happy? I can assure you both of the above neighbors believed that they were in the right, or they wouldn't have been willing to go to court and waste thousands of dollars. But were they happy? Can you imagine what

190

it would be like living next to someone who's watching every move you make, looking for evidence to use in court?

Being the person who reaches out doesn't mean you're wrong. What it means is you're willing to do your part in stopping the craziness.

What happens if they don't reach back? You have the satisfaction of giving it a try. And I can assure you if you don't try, it will only escalate. And one day, you'll find yourself saying, "How in the world did I get here?"

I was standing in line when a man in front of me said to his buddy, "You know my brother and I haven't spoken in thirty years. I just didn't like the way he treated our parents. He died last week. I wish I had made up with him before he died." It's terrible what our egos get us into.

2. What About Criticizers?

Earlier, we talked about gossiping. Now we're going to take up a form of gossiping, criticizing. We tend not to criticize our friends. Quite frankly, if we were critical of a friend, he wouldn't be our friend. But we find criticism runs rampant at parties and other social gatherings.

When someone is critical about someone else, it actually says more about the criticizer than the person being criticized. To criticize someone is an attempt to put the criticizer in a much more superior position.

When we say, "John is sure a lazy person," what we're also saying without using the actual words is, "Being lazy is a bad characteristic that I would never have in my life."

Think about it, how does criticism improve the world? It doesn't help the person we're saying the critical things about because they're usually not there to hear the criticism. And if they were, do you think they would respond with "Thanks. I never knew that. I really appreciate your pointing out my flaws." Would you say that if someone criticized you? I know I would have a hard time saying thanks.

"My recently departed wife was one of the sweetest, dearest, most loving people that ever lived. And I came pretty close to telling her that a few times, too!"

To be able to criticize someone and have a positive outcome requires a special skill with diplomacy and a special relationship with the person being criticized. And those two conditions are few and far between.

To maintain a good relationship with friends and neighbors, it's best to refrain from criticism and instead show people tolerance and respect.

3. Don't Be Stingy About Your Compliments

How often does someone give you a compliment? How often do you give a compliment to someone else?

Obviously, I think my wife, Sunny, is a magnificent person, and part of the evidence of that magnificence is that she regularly compliments people she encounters about an item of their attire or something they did.

I find it amazing the reaction she gets. Their face lights up with a smile, they stand straighter, and their entire countenance changes. The only down side is—if one can call it a down side—they may spend up to five minutes explaining the history of the item complimented or why they do the action complimented.

When it comes to complementing, we more often say something like, he or she doesn't need to hear me compliment them. They already know they do a good job. Or if I compliment them, they'll just get conceited.

We've all heard about people doing "random acts of kindness." And maybe we've even thought about doing some ourselves, but we've been reluctant because it may be costly or inconvenient. Here's a way to do a random act of kindness that doesn't cost anything and isn't inconvenient.

Make it a commitment to, once a day, give someone a compliment about an item of their attire or something you've just seen them do. And most service people have easily viewable name tags. So it's easy to add their name at the beginning of the compliment.

How much trouble is it to say, "Judy, that broach is really neat. Is it a family heirloom?" And then be amazed at how quickly you become the person's best friend. I'll bet you'll also receive outstanding service from them.

Incidentally, you'll probably end up getting as much pleasure from giving the compliment as the recipient and end up doing it more and more.

Just think what life would be like if we spent more time complimenting people and less time criticizing.

Incidentally, giving people compliments is actually a form of encouragement. And it's unbelievable what happens when we encourage people.

A group of frogs were traveling through the woods when two of them fell into a deep hole. All the other frogs gathered around the hole and saw how deep it was.

The two frogs tried jumping out of the hole, but they couldn't make it to the top. Each time they fell back to the bottom, hurting themselves.

The other frogs realized the hole was too deep to jump out and yelled to them that they were as good as dead.

Still the two frogs in the hole kept trying to jump out. Finally, as a result of the insistence from the other frogs that they could never make it out, one frog quit trying, lay down, and died.

The other frog continued jumping, in spite of what his friends were saying. Each time he jumped harder and finally made it out.

The successful frog continued jumping because he was deaf and couldn't hear what his friends were saying. He actually thought his fellow frogs were encouraging him the whole time.

> There is the power of life and death in the tongue.
>
> —Proverbs 18:2

4. Blow a Stranger's Mind

Has it ever amazed you when you're walking through a business parking lot, the people you encounter look down or in the opposite direction so as not to have to look at you as if you're the one who looks away?

Why is this? Chances are the people who do this are not happy. Any person who is happy holds their head high and shoulders back and has a smile on their face.

I know you're one of the happy people, so why not make one of these "eyeball avoiders" a bit happier or maybe even blow their mind.

When you pass them, say something similar to "Hello there. How are you doing?" I've done it on several occasions. Every time it brings them out of their trance, and it gives me a kick.

An elderly man came to live with his son, daughter-in-law, and young grandson. The elderly man was quite feeble, and his hands shook. During meals, it was not unusual for food to spill from the old man's fork or spoon. As he drank, the liquid would run down the corners of his mouth.

After a short time, the son could no longer take the mess that happened at each meal. He placed a small table in another room for the old man. To make sure he didn't break any dishes, the old man's food was placed in a wooden bowl. The old man became sad but accepted the new arrangements.

A few days after the old man had been moved into another room, the father noticed his son carving on a piece of wood with a table knife. The father asked his son what he was doing. His son replied, "I'm making wooden bowls for you and mom to eat from when you get old."

We must always remember that the way we treat others sets the standard for the way we are to be treated.

Chapter 10

Where Do We Go from Here?

Living a life in accordance with these seven principles won't guarantee financial prosperity, but I can assure you living by these principles will fill your life with happiness, and you will be surrounded by loving friends.

Our brain is a magnificent instrument. If injured, it has the ability to regenerate itself or assign other parts to assume the tasks of the injured part. Some scientists have said that we use only about 2 percent of our brain's capacity. Our brain can not only learn, it can be trained.

When Isaac Newton was asked how he discovered gravity, he replied, "By thinking about it all the time."

Like Newton, we also can make possible whatever it is we feel is important by using our brain and thinking about it all the time.

Keep in mind billions of dollars are spent each year, trying to convince us of the merits of a product or service. Virtually everything we have and use is the result of advertising. The soap you use for your laundry is the result of being bombarded with advertisements, no matter how much the advertisement irritated you at first.

Every day of your life, people are trying to sell you something. That product may not be a box of soap or an automobile but an idea. Their idea. Your boss, spouse, friend, and children all have their product or idea they want you to buy into. Sometimes, it's a legitimate idea. Your boss wants you to phone a customer about an order. Your child is hungry and wants you to feed him. Sometimes, they're not. Your boss wants you to lie to that customer about the dependability of the product you're trying to sell him. Your child is hungry for a candy bar thirty minutes before dinner.

> "If you haven't established a strong moral standard, someone else is going to make you fit into theirs."

Whether it's a product or an idea, you can be convinced to buy anything if you don't have a clear concept of what you believe. If you haven't established a strong moral standard, someone else is going to make you fit into theirs.

At the same time, a favorite way to protect ourselves is to close our minds to new ideas and thoughts. This way, we're left to think only about those ideas and thoughts that make us feel mentally safe. Since we're used to the old ways of thinking, we won't feel vulnerable by processing new information. We keep new information out of our awareness when it disagrees or conflicts with what we already have in mind.

It's always easier for us to shut out new information than to change our minds and viewpoints. As a closed-minded person, we'll remain safe in our own little mental world. However, this fear of changing our minds, ourselves, and our lifestyles will result in our missing out on what we could otherwise have.

It's difficult following these seven principles. Let me tell you, I've been trying ever since I came up with them several years ago. At the end of each day, I review what happened and how I put or didn't put these principles into practice. And I find every day I goof up. My goofing up doesn't discourage me because I have no allusions that I'm perfect. In reality, my reviewing my mistakes points out where improvement is needed, and as a result, I'm not aimlessly going through the day.

What follows are ideas on how to be successful in inaugurating "the code" in our lives.

Practice Makes Perfect

My father used to say, "Practice makes perfect." Basketball legend Larry Bird used to spend hours shooting the basketball from awkward positions. Supposedly, he wasn't an extremely talented player. But in a game, he made some of the most astounding shots in some of the most awkward positions. Why? Because that was what he practiced.

When a person practices anything, they enhance their attitude by knowing they can do it. They can say to themselves, "I've done it before, and I can do it again."

At the same time, one must be careful not to let a failure develop the attitude of failure in us. We can accept the fact that we failed, but we need to say to ourselves, "I may have failed before, but I'll find a way to do it again."

Although the thoughts and recommendations in this book were written by me, they came from literally thousands of sources and people.

These are concepts that others have found successful. But they do no good unless we use them. And like the unbelievable shots Larry Bird made, he had to take them in order to make them. And he had to practice them in order to have the confidence to take them.

"The thoughts and recommendations in this book came from thousands of sources and people."

To stay with the analogy, the ball is in our court. We can close the cover to this book and continue our life as it has been or we can practice the ideas and eventually they'll become as natural to us as breathing.

And as I indicated about my following the principles above, don't be discouraged. Be excited that you still have the ability to grow.

It could just very well be the distance you have to grow may seem like crossing the Grand Canyon or even eating that elephant we talked about in Chapter 7. So, once again, how do you eat an elephant? You eat an elephant one bite at a time. Any time we're faced with an awesome task, the task needs to be broken down into pieces and attacked one piece at a time.

In living by the code, there is a natural breakdown of bites. As a matter of fact, there are seven bites—each of the principles. So what you need to do is look at the seven principles and select the one that intrigues you the most. Then work to make it a part of your life. As you swallow each bite, you'll find it gives you a success that will nourish you and give you more energy for the next bite.

If You Don't Start, You Can't Finish

One of the fundamental facts of life is if you don't start, you don't stand a chance of getting there. It sounds simple and seems obvious. But still, it's a major factor in why we don't do what we know we should do. Some people call it the paralysis of analysis. It's easy to sit in the comfort of our status quo and rationalize about what we could or should do if we had more information or if circumstances were just different. Successful people take action. If Sister Teresa hadn't picked up that first orphaned child, she would have never picked up the thousands that followed.

> "If Sister Teresa hadn't picked up that first orphaned child, she would have never picked up the thousands that followed."

To use another analogy: It's a fact of baseball; a player can't steal second if he keeps one foot on first base.

According to Wayne Dyer, "You'll seldom experience regret for anything that you've done. It's what you haven't done that will torment you. The message, therefore, is clear. Do it! Develop an appreciation for the present moment. Seize every second of your life and savor it. Value your present moments. Using them up in any self-defeating ways means you've lost them forever."

There have been a number of magical moments in my life. One of them was back when Sunny and I lived in California. I was beginning to get overwhelmed with work and all the pressures of life. We decided to escape it all by taking a long weekend off and renting a cabin along a river in the woods. The cabin was made of rocks and absolutely quant and restful. But the magical part of the weekend was an embroidered and framed saying on one of the walls of the kitchen. I wrote it down and immediately started applying it to my life. I can tell you, when I went back to the pressures of my life, this saying put them in prospective, and I literally started looking forward to what I could accomplish and not dreading what I had to endure. Here is that saying:

"This is the beginning of a new day.
God has given me this day to use as I will.
I can waste it or use it for good.
What I do today is very important because
I am exchanging a day of my life for it.
When tomorrow comes, this day will be gone forever
Leaving something in its place I have traded for it.
I want it to be gain, not loss . . .
good, not evil . . .
success, not failure
in order that I shall not regret the price I paid for it.

Just How Determined Are You?

No one can obtain anything of significance without a high level of dedication to that accomplishment.

Julius Caesar was very much aware of this fact. When his armies invaded England by ship, he wanted to make sure his men understood the only two options were victory or death. What did he do? He burned all their ships in front of his army.

Back in 1999, when Sunny and I started our monthly publication, *Chronicle of the Old West*, we both quit our legitimate jobs with great salaries, expense accounts, and paid vacations before the first edition was published. That's burning our ships.

I'm not requesting this level of commitment to living by "the code"; however, no one can do his best as long as he knows that if the battle gets too tough, he's saved a way to retreat.

"But," we say, "what if people think I'm being 'holier than thou'?" And then what happens when they see me do something that isn't in accordance with "the code?"

We're all contractors. What do we build? We build bridges—bridges we never cross. Mark Twain said, "I've been through some terrible things in my life, some of which actually happened."

How many times have we worried about something for days, only to have it take place and find our worries were for nothing?

If we're going to encounter something over which we have no control, why worry about it? There's nothing we can do. If we're going to encounter something over which we have control, why worry about it? We're in control.

We're all familiar with the Ten Commandments. There is another commandment that's mentioned in the Bible much more than these ten combined. The commandment is "fear not." It's mentioned 366 times—once for every day of the year, with leap year thrown in for good measure.

It's interesting that when a person is thoroughly committed, that person doesn't see the obstacles that someone without that level of commitment will find devastating.

A young man moved from the city to a small town. Because most people in the town had horses, he decided to purchase one for himself. Unfortunately, he didn't have enough land to keep the horse at his home, so he decided to board the horse elsewhere.

At the first stable, the owner said the cost for room and board was $100 per month, and the owner of the horse would get to take home all the manure the horse created. The second stable owner said his charge was $75, and the owner could have all the manure. The third person said his cost was $50 but said nothing about manure.

"What about the manure?" asked the owner of the horse.

Responded the stable owner, "At $50, there is no manure."

What you get out of something is totally dependent on what you put into it.

Develop a Plan

Steven Covey in *The Seven Habits of Highly Effective People* says, "It's incredibly easy to get caught up in an activity trap, in the busy-ness of life, to work harder and harder at climbing the ladder of success only to discover it's leaning against the wrong wall."

Successful businesses understand that in order for them to be successful, they have to keep their ultimate objective in mind, so daily decisions will be made in accordance with that ultimate objective or mission.

"Heroes come in all shapes and sizes."

Lewis Walker, former president of the Institute of Certified Planners, says the greatest obstacle to people's success is fuzzy goals. Mr. Walker explains fuzzy goals as a person saying that someday he or she wants to have a cabin in the mountains. It isn't a specific goal, and therefore, not likely to happen.

> "The greatest obstacle to people's success is fuzzy goals."

A specific goal is when you find the mountain, draw up plans for the cabin, find out how much it will cost with inflation figured in to the date you want to occupy it, and how much money you'll need to save per month to have the cabin.

The cabin has now moved from a wish to a goal with a plan to accomplish it.

Get Friends to Join You in This Project

Synergism is the ability of two or more to achieve an effect of which each is individually incapable. Napoleon Hill, author of *Think and Grow Rich*, used the concept of synergism in what he called a mastermind group. By two or more people of a similar mind getting together and talking, an additional mind is created, which is much more powerful than the total of all the minds in the group. Mr. Hill discovered that all the over two hundred successful people he interviewed used the concept of synergism. And for every successful person, that continues to be true to this day.

That synergism can be created with a small group of friends, business associates, or family. The importance is that each person be of a similar mind.

Our Heroes

When I was a kid growing up, I had my heroes. Two who were at the top of my list were Roy Rogers and Hopalong Cassidy. Each of these men understood the influence they had on people, and they represented what was good about America: strength, principle, and decency. Both of them actually had a code of life that they asked people to live by. In case you don't remember them or are too young to remember them, here they are:

Roy Rogers Rider's Club Rules

1. Be neat and clean.
2. Be courteous and polite.
3. Always obey your parents.
4. Protect the weak and help them.
5. Be brave but never take chances.
6. Study hard and learn all you can.
7. Be kind to animals and take care of them.
8. Eat all your food and never waste any.
9. Love God and go to Sunday school regularly.
10. Always respect our flag and our country.

Hopalong Cassidy's Creed for American Boys and Girls

1. The highest badge of honor a person can wear is honesty. Be truthful at all times.
2. Your parents are the best friends you have. Listen to them, and obey their instructions.
3. If you want to be respected, you must respect others. Show good manners in every way.
4. Only through hard work and study, can you succeed. Don't be lazy.
5. Your good deeds always come to light. So don't boast or be a show-off.
6. If you waste time or money today, you will regret it tomorrow. Practice thrift in all ways.
7. Many animals are good and loyal companions. Be friendly and kind to them.
8. A strong, healthy body is a precious gift. Be neat and clean.
9. Our country's laws are made for your protection. Observe them carefully.
10. Children in many foreign lands are less fortunate than you are. Be glad and proud you are an American.

Many a young person had these creeds in their room, and when they didn't know what to do, they would ask what would Roy or Hoppy do?

Many Christians do something similar today. They live by the principle WWJD (What Would Jesus Do?).

Roy Rogers made eighty-seven movies. He was in a strange position in that he was not only a person, he was a character. When Roy had a question about how to do a movie or TV scene, the real Roy Rogers would ask himself what Roy Rogers, the character, would do.

"When undecided, the real Roy Rogers would ask himself what Roy Rogers, the character, would do."

What do you think would happen if one of today's heroes, movie stars and professional athletes, were to come out with a similar code? They would literally be crucified. What professional football player Tim Tebow says is mild compared to Roy Rogers and Hopalong Cassidy, and look what happens to him.

Heroes are important to a child's development. Heroes convey the best of what society has to offer. They influence the choices children make and shape a child's moral foundation.

Who are today's heroes? As indicated earlier, they're movie stars and professional athletes. They're the ones in front of children virtually every day as they watch TV, go to movies, and read magazines.

I'm not going to beat up on them for not being good examples because I believe retired Phoenix Sun's basketball player Charles Barkley spoke for most movie stars and professional athletes when he said, "I am not a role model." I believe the vast majority would echo Charles.

Hardly a day goes by that we don't see, hear, or read a news item about a movie star or professional athlete being arrested on drug, alcohol, or battery charges.

Recently, I saw a news item on TV about a Hollywood couple getting a divorce. After the news anchor delivered the report, the co-anchor said, "Well, they were married for a pretty long time, seven years."

In addition, another category of heroes that our young people look at for guidance is a group of people we put in the spotlight through the election process—our politicians. These people regularly show unheroic activities like dishonesty, irresponsibility, and greed.

But you say, I didn't elect them, and they're a member of the other political party. No political party or conservative or liberal persuasion has a monopoly on corruption. We have to watch when we put political position above ethics. When our young people see someone whom we've supported do something unethical or illegal and we don't take a stand in opposition to what they did, people who know we've supported that person may just feel we also support their unethical or illegal action.

Where Are Today's Heroes?

So where are today's real heroes? I regularly hear people say all our heroes are gone. It may be that Roy Rogers and Hopalong Cassidy are dead, and for our younger generation, forgotten or more accurately, unknown. As great they were, they were a small element in America's heroism.

Who are the real heroes? You are. I am. We, not the politicians, not the famous, are the real heroes. We're the ones who make this great country successful. And we need to assert our position as heroes.

> **"Who are the real heroes? You are. I am."**

Our real heroes aren't the people whose mug shots we regularly see on television. Our heroes are the ordinary people who jump into action when there's a need. They're people who make a difference in other people's lives with less concern for their own.

Fortunately, we often hear of heroes like airline pilot "Sully" Sullenberger, who back on January 15, 2009, landed his plane on the Hudson River and saved his life, along with 155 passengers. And he was not only a hero then, but his actions since that event have proved himself to be a hero worth looking up to.

But most people go through their life, never being in a position similar to Sullenberger's.

That doesn't mean we're excused from being a hero. In order to be a hero, the first thing we need to do is to ask ourselves what our ideal hero would look like and how would he/she act. Then we should compare our vision of a hero with our own lives.

First, I can assure you, you'll feel you don't stack up to your image. That's OK. If you did feel you were the image of your hero, chances are excellent you're lying to yourself. None of us should feel we're the fulfillment of our hero, even though we might be a lot closer than we think. Because once we've arrived, life's challenges are over.

"We're not perfect, but if we try to give it our 'best shot' every day, we could be somebody's hero."

For the vast majority of people, their heroism is as a parent, teacher, husband/wife, employer/employee, neighbor/friend, or just being a person of character. And being a hero in these circumstances is extremely difficult because these positions are typically filled by ordinary people—people who make mistakes and forget things. And we want our heroes to be people who don't make mistakes and don't forget things. We choose people who are at a distance so we can imagine they're perfect, and they can easily be put on a pedestal.

We need to understand real heroes aren't the ones more commonly thought of as heroes, but this country's heroes are the ordinary people among us who live their lives quietly and when called for action, make a difference in people's lives.

The bottom line is America needs a new breed of heroes—people who live their lives based on precepts that call for the best in each of us. The basic fact is, "Heroes are made, not born."

"Heroes are made, not born."

A teacher asked her students to write a paper on how it would feel if they were an A+ student. After writing the paper, each of them started getting better grades.

Using that same principle, we need to ask ourselves if we were living our lives according to the code—how we would feel, what we would do, and even what we would look like and then live our lives accordingly. And when we do this, I can assure you, your life will change, and you will change the lives of others.

I recently heard a woman speak who had spent a number of years as a hospice worker. She said during those last few days of the lives of virtually everyone she worked with, they talked with regrets about the things they didn't do. My prayer is that when you and I come to the end of our lives, we'll be able to tell those around us how we made a difference.

May God always be at your side!

We truly hope this book has inspired you to make positive changes in your life.

If so, or if not, we would like to hear from you.

Our web site will not only give you an opportunity to express your thoughts, you will also be able to read what other people are saying and doing about living the code in their lives.

You will also have an opportunity to let us recognize someone in your life who has exemplified the code in their life.

Visit us at: *www.livingthecode.com*

CPSIA information can be obtained
at www.ICGtesting.com
Printed in the USA
FFHW02n0843231018
48943545-53175FF